DIRTBAG ASTROLOGY

ALBERTO TORIBIO

THE DIRTBAG ASTROLOGER

STERLING ETHOS
New York

STERLING ETHOS
New York

An Imprint of Sterling Publishing Co., Inc.

ISBN 978-1-4549-4552-9 (hardcover)

ISBN 978-1-4549-4553-6 (e-book)

Library of Congress Control Number: 2022933967

For information about custom editions, special sales, and premium
purchases, please contact specialsales@unionsquareandco.com.

Printed in the United States of America

2 4 6 8 10 9 7 5 3 1

unionsquareandco.com

Cover design by Melissa Farris

Interior design by Christine Heun

Cover credits:
Shutterstock.com: pp.ng (stars); Gorbash Varvara (hand, constellation)

Interior credits:
Creative Market: kaer_shop: throughout (letters), **iStock/Getty Images Plus:** Anastasiia
Kurman: throughout (orbital zodiac); Nerhuz: 176, **Shutterstock.com:** Chikovnaya: 10, 192;
Croisy: 9; E.Va: 116 (horoscope wheel); KK.KICKIN: throughout (starry sky); Gorbash Varvara:
throughout (hands, constellations, zodiac constellations, double moon, pyramid hands)

"Everybody has a secret world inside of them. I mean everybody . . . no matter how dull and boring they are on the outside. Inside them they've all got unimaginable, magnificent, wonderful, stupid, amazing worlds."

—Neil Gaiman, *A Game of You*

For my persevering Capricorn mom
and my tenacious Aquarius dad.

CONTENTS

PART 1 THE SUN
Our Soul Truth, Whether You Like It or Not

PART 2 THE MOON
Our Gooey Emotional Center

INTRODUCTION

"As above, so below." You've probably heard this saying before, maybe from a hippie auntie, a liberal arts major trying to show off how deep they are, or a friend who recently discovered Wicca. The saying, although often uttered in a whimsical tone, is meant to describe how our external world is very much influenced by the internal world. It is an ancient principle that is almost two thousand years old, although the idea of it is much more primordial and lingers within us when we are alone in the middle of the night. The origins of this principle don't really matter. When used with actual intention, the principle can shape our understanding of ourselves and our world. And, most importantly, it's our gateway into astrology. It means that whatever is happening to us is also reflected all around us. What is happening with the stars and the heavens is reflected back down to earth.

AS ABOVE

SO BELOW

Crop tops; potato-topped Korean corn dogs; watercolor eye shadow; contouring; and any trend that sparks on Twitter, TikTok, or Instagram—same thing, believe it or not. We see them and give them a like or whatever, but their reach doesn't end with just our initial reaction: they affect us and the people around us. Trends going on around us reflect the current climate of the population. The type of artist we gravitate toward reflects our psyche. The macro is a reflection of the micro, and we are all just an echo of something or someone else's influence.

WHAT IS ASTROLOGY?

But don't worry, that doesn't mean you don't have any autonomy or a will of your own. Necessarily. It just means all of us are affected by everything and everyone that touches our reality. Like Oscar Wilde said, "Most people are other people, their thoughts are someone else's opinions, their lives a mimicry." And if you're offended, slow down. It isn't wrong to want a safe and vanilla life. It isn't a bad thing to be easily influenced by whatever wave of culture is going right now—to only listen to Top 40. To live in a bubble of safety and comfort. Unfortunately, life has never been safe and sound. If you are someone like me, who wasn't born with much privilege in your favor, or you are someone who is looking for more ways to take advantage of life, you might want to look to a Higher Power to make sense of everything going on in the world. And that's fine.

Like the psychologist Carl Jung hypothesized, every religion comes from the same source, the collective unconscious. The collective unconscious represents our unified understanding of symbols and meaning, something Jung believed was innate to our individual psyches. This is why even cultures that are far apart from one another can share a basic understanding that the moon is tied to femininity, emotions, and cycles. It is why people understand that when the moon is full, people's most wild emotions, and even madness, come to the surface. It is why different systems of divination like tarot, Lenormand, scrying, tea leaf reading, and more can all bring you answers from the collective unconscious. But there is a different system that can add meaning to your days, and astrology is part of that system: an interconnected web that moves us and the events around us. And if you're reading this book, maybe you don't want a cookie-cutter life. Maybe you want to grab a surfboard, stay above the water, and navigate the waves of culture and influence going on in the world. But honestly, you need to listen to the weather report to anticipate the climate. This book is an opportunity for you to tune in and make an educated guess about whether rain is coming. If you're headed to the beach, buckle up—the following chapters will give you an idea of what's coming in your life; what you do with that information is up to you.

Astrology is the cosmic study of the movements and conversations the celestial bodies have with one another. Whatever the stars do, wherever they are, and whoever they come in contact with, the energy is mirrored back at us both personally and in the public consciousness. And if that definition makes you yawn, remember: astrology is also an ultimate weapon that can help you destroy your enemies, get laid, and dismantle the psychic monsters of this world. It's a way of seeing the universe, an occult tool for guessing the future, and it's also a way to start a conversation with someone you met at a bar. It's all of these things; but in order for you to have a holistic comprehension of it and also learn what a deep resource it can be for existential understanding, try to listen to the explanation in the next paragraph.

The first astrologers were farmers who took note of the moons and the stars. They were able to predict the weather, tell time, and anticipate the change in the air based on their observations. A little farther into the future, and each phase of the moon began to gain more artistic and esoteric meaning. The sun, which started as a simple way to anticipate physical changes in the environment, became a symbol of our consciousness. The moon, which was originally just a time-keeping tool, became a symbol of our inner emotional world. Obviously, we are going to skip over almost the entire history of astrology, but this progression is the most important thing you need to know about the ways in which humans have interacted with astrological thought. Now I'm going to tell you about the basics of astrology, because if you are reading this book, you want to know how you can use astrology to take advantage of your life.

I believe that astrology is a tool not of faith, but of free will. A tool to help enlightened individuals. So many billionaires, gays, and teenagers are into astrology in the twenty-first century. This is because they, too—like the farmers before them—see patterns and synchronicities that unfold through celestial movements. They understand that there are psychic undercurrents that connect and affect us all. They also like memes and enjoy justifying their actions based on their Sun and Moon signs, and/or whether Mercury is in retrograde. Which is valid, although obviously if you take the time to dig into the qualities of your Sun and Moon signs, and the actual machinations of Mercury retrograde, you'll know a lot more about this world.

Take Mercury retrograde, for example: it's a buzz word, but it also describes a complex astrological event. And even if you don't know everything about it, you can feel it if you're sensitive to what's going on in your environment. It takes someone with a sensitivity to the world around them to see that when Mercury goes retrograde, the whole world seems to be falling apart. If they look closer, they may see ghosts from their past coming back all at once: and if you learn about Mercury retrograde, you'll begin to understand that it is a period of time that's perfect for rethinking the choices you have made in your life. Some people—I, for example, am one of them—are self-aware enough to see that they attract the same type of person, but not smart enough to understand why—or to grow from it. But through astrology, you can gain the language to understand your love language and make more thoughtful choices.

You want to know where your soul truth lies? How to take advantage of your work life? How to have everyone in the room fall in love with your presence? When you might fall in love? Or just how to gain the respect of your enemies? Astrology has so many of the answers you might need—or at the least the information to give you a psychic, conscious understanding of how life works—to get you a step ahead in this world.

A NOTE FROM THE DIRTBAG ASTROLOGER

As you begin reading this book, you may be asking: Why Sun and Moon only? No rising signs? No transits? Where are all the planets?! And houses?! And to that, I say, Please slow your roll. This is just the barest hint of wisdom from your friendly neighborhood astrologer, meant to get your appetite going for a more comprehensive banquet. Which is to say: Sun signs are the core of who we are. Moon signs are the squishy emotional underbelly. And this handbook should give you an initial way to get to know yourself, your Tinder date, your sister, your mom, your shittiest boss. I hope you enjoy, and I hope this gives you what you need so you can get to know the people around you in a more comprehensive way—horrifying details and all.

PART 1

THE SUN

OUR SOUL TRUTH, WHETHER YOU LIKE IT OR NOT

WHEN WE LOOK AT ASTROLOGY AS A TOOL to learn more about ourselves, we must first look at our natal chart, also called the birth or star chart. The Sun is perhaps our most important planetary body. And in astrology, it's the star of the show— the symbol of life, happiness, hope, and inspiration. When we look at our horoscope, we usually look at our Sun sign, the sign the Sun was in when we were born, whether we understand anything about our birth chart or not. And if you do have some background and learn how to read your natal chart or anything in more depth, forget the esoteric history of it all. To get straight to the point, we find our soul in the Sun. It shows us our sense of self, our core personality, what we will strive to become.

SUN SIGNS: What Are They?

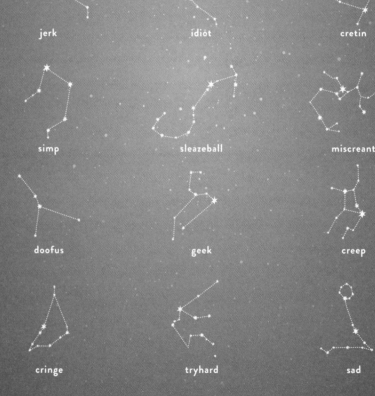

jerk

idiot

cretin

simp

sleazeball

miscreant

doofus

geek

creep

cringe

tryhard

sad

Sun signs, as noted above, are the core of our personality. Yes, it's totally fine to identify with being a Leo, a Gemini, or whatever. You may not know anything about your astrological truth, but that is fine—and it's a pretty good start. Gather your astrology-related memes and pull up a chair. We're going to start with a little background about the Sun, so you'll know at least a tiny bit before we dig into the twelve zodiac signs. Or at least feel justified in assuming an air of authority when you tell someone they're "such an Aries."

Of course, in astrology we don't call the Sun a planet—it is a luminary. If we look at the astrological glyph of the Sun, ⊙, we see a circle with a dot in the middle. The circle represents the universe, every atom, every bird, every cloud, every living being, every rock, every bit of stardust that exists, every bit of stardust that has ever existed, it has no end or beginning; it is the void of endless possibilities and pure inspiration. The dot in the middle of the glyph represents the manifestation, the unknown, the life that has sprouted from the universe; it is where ideas are born and the culmination of where new individuals are born. It's a beautiful and simple representation of how we sprouted from nothing into the people we are today, as well as how we are also a culmination of everything that is around us, the appreciation that we are all part of something bigger.

So, yes, you're a special and beautiful snowflake. Just like the Sun is the center of our universe, the Sun in our own astrological chart is the center of our own personal universe. Every other celestial body draws its energy and adds to it. But though we are all special and unique in our own perception, astrology also teaches us to have an outlook where we are all not too different from one another. Yup, sorry—we are all much more alike than we like to think. When you were born, there were ten thousand other people who were born at the exact same time as you, perhaps in a country on the other side of the world or just a town over; and although it may change the need for those planets, their essences are the same as yours. But don't freak out: although you may share the same birthday or the same Sun sign as someone else, there are other factors that make you different from someone born a day after or even a few minutes before you. Whether you feel attached to your Sun sign or not, you and everyone born under the same sign share a basic soul truth. For example: all Sagittarians are searching for a spiritual truth, Capricorns are building on a legacy, and Geminis are all students of life. Cancers are unpacking their mommy issues, Leos are trying hard to be the center of the universe, and Libras are trying to figure out how to have the perfect relationship.

So, if you're ever looking for the answer to what will give your life meaning, you should look at your Sun sign to contrast the path your life has taken with the soul journey that your zodiac sign expresses. We eventually grow into our Sun sign, as we find our own individuality and accept the structure and direction that it gives us, or we stay away from it, trying to find something new that will make us feel whole. Either way, I like to think we eventually find our meaning and purpose. Some of us will take a longer time figuring it out—or we can simply read the next section of this book and sign up willingly for whatever reason-for-being your Sun sign is all about.

ARIES SUN

MARCH 21–APRIL 19

ARCHETYPE: The baby, the one who keeps it real, the hothead

MODALITY: Cardinal

ELEMENT: Fire

HOUSE: 1st (physicality, conscious thought, personality and presentation)

ANATOMY: Head, eyes, face

RULER: Mars

ESOTERIC RULER: Mercury

QUOTE: "Life is too short to ask for forgiveness."

In the beginning, the universe started off as nothing but a vast space of emptiness—just like my brain when I had to sit down and write a school report, or days in the summer when I had nothing to do but stare at the ceiling or a blank piece of paper. Then suddenly there was a word, a bang, chaos. A spark of inspiration came and turned that blank piece of paper into a painting, motivation came and got me typing away, and my boring summer day got interrupted by a Tinder match asking me out on a date. Aries is that: the energy that ignites the universe.

When we look at astrology, we have to view it as a story. Aries is the beginning, the baby, the first. Yet in some ways every beginning marks the end of something. A blank piece of paper is just that until you push a pen across it.

Aries is the first move. Aries is an explosion. Fireworks are nothing and do nothing until a spark lights the fuse and causes it to illuminate the dark and empty night sky. But, all that poetry aside, there is no real meaning to fireworks. They're just instant gratification—things that light up and go boom. Aries is the same thing: all about the moment.

In astrology, each planet captures an energy of the human experience. For example, the emotion of rage and passion: it's an energy that is captured by the planet Mars. Yet not everyone channels those emotions the same way, and that's when we start looking into what sign the planets are in to see how those emotions will be channeled. With how distinct the personalities of each sign are, the planets' energy either flows easily or has trouble being in their own energy. For example: the planet Venus hates being in Scorpio because the planet isn't about deep emotions or transformation. Venus is a planet of beauty, money, and love. This planet is trying to have an easy time and enjoy the luxuries of life; she's not trying to be intense or deep. Mars hates being in Libra because it doesn't want to think about finding a middle ground; you are in the midst of a war. As for the Sun, it loves being in Aries.

The Sun in astrology is all about the self, soul, ego, the father. It is the "I am" planet, and Aries is the literal embodiment of "I am." Aries doesn't like answering to other people. They don't like other people getting more attention than they do. You think Leos are narcissistic? Well, you haven't met Aries. Leo's vanity is harmless. Leo overthinks things and obsesses about themselves through the culture and the people in their immediate community—they're endlessly fixated on how others see them. Aries, on the other hand, views life through their own perspective first and foremost. Everything is about them. Just like other Fire signs, they are mythomaniacs. These people are obsessed with curating and keeping up with the mythos they came up with in their head—think Mariah Carey. These people view themselves as the center of their own show and will pounce on you the minute you disrupt their perception.

With Aries being the first sign, they are also the baby of the Zodiac. So, like a baby, Aries is naturally self-centered, lively, energetic, unapologetic, a ball of passion. Aries pukes, cries, and otherwise lets loose liberally and without self-consciousness. One of the most redeeming qualities they possess is that they view and treat the world like it is the "first time." When they fall in love, they treat it like it's the first time. When they talk to a new person, they treat the experience like it's fascinating and revelatory—like this is the first person they have ever talked to. They are forever young and full of energy and can be magnetic and fascinating. But, like a baby, small child, or untrained dog, they can also be infuriating.

Aries is a cardinal sign, which is all about action and initiation. Ruled by Mars, a planet of action and aggression, Aries is known for being reckless, fearless, and action oriented. They tend not to think twice before they engage. As a sign ruled by the element of Fire, which is aligned with passion and inspiration, they tend to start things and never finish them. Going on a spontaneous date the same day they started talking with someone? They would absolutely go for it but might not go for a second date. Hook up with people they meet at a party? They have no moral qualms about it but will kick them out immediately after hooking up. They will gladly tell you they're in love first and start bailing out once the excitement is over. Haunted houses? They will gladly go to investigate it to see if the rumors are true, bailing out twelve seconds after going in. Aries is a sign that follows the passion but isn't the most reliable to keep the fire lasting; that's the job of a Leo. Aries likes to march to the beat of their own drum, but they don't know where that sound is going to take them. Also, they have no regard for whether you are trying to work during that drum practice, and if you try to stop them from playing, they will absolutely freak out.

Aries has been stealing hearts since they were born, but getting their heart stolen is another story entirely. Because Aries is so "me!" oriented, you have to make a bold first impression to get their interest. Naturally competitive and ready for a fight, they like people who will be a challenge to pursue or those who are very direct. To get their attention, you might as well be a real jerk: be a show-off and throw your best self at them, or they might not be interested. Give them your best joke, tell them how pretty they are, and don't be afraid to give them flowers—just don't send them an anonymous love letter. Subtlety's not really their thing. If you have a crush on them and you ever feel lost about their intentions, there is a real chance they are not interested or just can't take a hint. Aries is not the type of person who likes to play games, so they will always let you know how they feel right away. If by any chance they do tell you they aren't interested, stand tall and let them know the treasure that you are. Aries will fall for someone with an ego bigger than their own—so that's a good last-ditch effort or at least a way to make them want you while you walk away.

In astrology, the Sun represents the individual and their path to being a complete person. Aries is learning to form their own individuality. Going off on adventures to expand their views, fighting for the things that make life worth living for, and leaping into anything that challenges who they are—all very Aries occupations. Aries likes it intense and exciting, and Aries thinks they *are* intense and exciting. Aries will spend all their life being amazed by themselves. The good part here is that Aries is optimistic, and they are a sign of faith. They came into this world—at least in the sense of esoteric astrology—with no prior experience. They leap into the universe eager to see the next thing and need no prior knowledge or understanding to enjoy anything this life has or will offer.

TAURUS SUN

APRIL 20–MAY 20

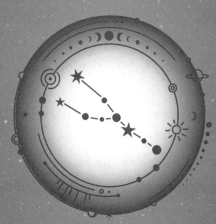

ARCHETYPE: The Material Girl, the hedonist, the most stubborn person in the world

MODALITY: Fixed

ELEMENT: Earth

HOUSE: 2nd (values, self-worth, security, natural talent)

ANATOMY: Throat

RULER: Venus

ESOTERIC RULER: Vulcan

QUOTE: "I'm super chill and flexible! But also, if you buy the cheap toilet paper, I will literally die."

ries is the initiator who births new life, and Taurus comes right after that to keep life growing. In Aries, we learn about the "I am." Taurus's key phrase is "I have." So you can already tell they're a bit possessive about things, but they're not a cheapskate or a miser. Taurus naturally rules the part of the chart that is all about wealth, self-worth, security, possessions, and natural strength. If all the zodiacs were to sit around a table in chronological order, Aries would be the main character and Taurus would be the right-hand man. Taurus is an Earth sign, so they tend to be practical and realistic people. They place value in life and on things they can actually hold on to physically, things that are tied to reality.

Ruled by Venus, the goddess of beauty, Taurus takes after the more sensual aspects of the planet. They are horny people, they are hedonistic, they enjoy good wine as much as they love having sex. Taurus reminds us to enjoy what we have in front of us. While Aries is busy trying to find themselves and jumps from one adventure to the next, Taurus has already mastered the art of being themselves. Taurus is enjoying the things they can have, grow, and gain more of—this lifetime is for surrounding themselves with whatever it is that makes them happy.

Taurus is the first of the three Earth signs, meaning that it's the least developed in its element. Tauruses naturally seek to build on the things they value, but they don't necessarily go deep. Sometimes Tauruses can get so caught up in gathering things and satisfying their earthly senses that they forget to develop their spiritual body. Several thousand dollars' worth of shoes in the closet at any given time? With the proper resources, absolutely. A wealth of spiritual knowledge from years of study? Not necessarily. Still, Karl Marx was a Taurus who spent his whole life revolutionizing and getting people to rethink how they looked at wealth and labor. As a mature Taurus, he understood that wealth wasn't evenly distributed and some people were willing to exploit and take away from others to satisfy their own greed. A highly functional Taurus might understand that accumulation of wealth and luxury is an empty indulgence and can even cross the line into sin when it can't be sustained and when the people around them are starving and don't even have basic necessities. But does every Taurus get there? Nope!

In the tarot, Taurus takes after the Hierophant, represented by a priestlike figure. You might be thinking to yourself "What does this old man have in common with the Goddess of Beauty?" It's true that Taurus's gorgeous and sensual ruling planet is somewhat at odds with the old dude in the hat. But both archetypes remind us that, as humans, we have this eternal instinct to put value and meaning into our lives.

Tauruses are stubborn, fixed in their ways, grumpy about the slightest changes, and are the last people to ever leave a fight. Acquisitive and unbalanced Tauruses are constantly possessed by the desire to own everything they can get their hands on. They are known to gravitate toward worldly objects that give them meaning and joy. Tauruses look into the material world for fulfillment. They are said to be sentimental or emotional hoarders who seek to collect items of wealth that will give meaning and worth to their lives. They personify their items, treating their cars like actual babies, seeking physical pleasure to relieve themselves of existential demons. Yet they are the most loyal, and their solid values remind us that some things in this life are worth fighting for and seeing through to the end.

However, not all Tauruses are too certain where they can place their value. They can get lost in their passions and even make the leap to full-on fanaticism as they try to justify and hold on to things that keep them grounded, even when that no longer serves them. However, some things aren't meant to be held on to or seen through until the end. That goes for treasured toys and old clothes, crappy jobs, relationships that have been toxic for a long time. Taurus is the girl with the terrible boyfriend but who just can't quite leave him. Taurus complains about his boss every time you meet him for a drink but won't seek a better opportunity elsewhere. Taurus is that person who will always be around.

Change is always inevitable in this world. People die, items get stolen, friends backstab, romances flourish, feelings change, governments fall. When the world is full of uncertainty, we have to learn to let go and find better value systems when we realize the ones we have are no longer working as they should. If there is anything a Taurus needs to know to live a full life, it's to learn how to let go, burn the failed parts of their life to the ground, and work on building something better. A Taurus says "I have," but sometimes they should say "I quit" instead.

There is a preciousness in understanding the value of things both physical and nonphysical, and a balanced Taurus will be able to treasure his awesome car, his great house, his shoe collection, or whatever without becoming freakishly obsessed and fixated on those possessions. He will also have a healthy life full of fulfilling relationships, an intellectually stimulating occupation, maybe even volunteer work that gives him the satisfaction of helping others. Or, you know, at least he can be "no thoughts, head empty" in a really nice way that satisfies him without the addiction of acquisitiveness. A balanced Taurus will be able to enjoy his nights with a glass of Dom Pérignon in one hand and an Air Jordan III OG in the other, surrounded by friends he loves and romantic partners he lavishes with time and gifts. Or, if he's unbalanced, he might die alone, crushed by the loneliness that comes from working and building superficial wealth with no one to share it with. It just depends on how a Taurus interprets the central lesson of his life: how to balance his love of things with a realistic concept of their value.

When it comes to romance, Tauruses are very much about following their gut instincts. They value their emotions and get swept away by the gravity of their own hearts when they feel things deeply. But believe it or not, they are really picky when it comes to romance. Not just anyone will do it for them. They look and seek out a crush that keeps them up late into the night. They want to love hard. If you have a crush on a Taurus, there are a few things you can try: buy them flowers, give them macarons, or get them some stationery items (really anything they can use every day, since they like to surround themselves with little luxuries). But there's not much you can do to get a Taurus if you're not attractive. So, #1 tip: Just be hot. You can shower Taurus with gifts and praise, but ultimately—just be hot. At their best, Taurus is the most emotionally evolved of the zodiac and seeks someone who can see through them and uncover what's underneath their bullish exterior, so there's still a chance if your emotional connection is electrifying. And if all else fails, just buy a Taurus a Gucci bag—they can't resist luxury gifts.

GEMINI SUN

MAY 21–JUNE 20

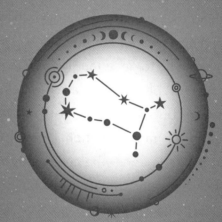

ARCHETYPE: The trickster, the exhausting conversationalist, the charming asshole

MODALITY: Mutable

ELEMENT: Air

HOUSE: 3rd (siblings, relatives, neighborhood, primary school, writing, literature, transportation)

ANATOMY: Lungs, nervous system

RULER: Mercury

ESOTERIC RULER: Venus

QUOTE: "You're boring, so I'm going to go now, but this was awesome. Bye!"

*L*et's get right into talking about one of the most controversial signs in the zodiac, the Twins, also known as Gemini. Charming, quick, smart, and fun, Gemini lives to talk, to learn, to communicate—they are the embodiment of the element of Air. They have a million niche interests. They could not imagine a life where they aren't trying to gain higher truths and have fun while doing it. But they are also popularly known as the jerks of the zodiac: they will question your intent about everything, from the tone of your voice to the type of shoes you decided to wear that day. These people are prone to spiraling easily; they aren't the most grounded and have a constant thirst to make sense of everything and figure out why things are the way they are.

Gemini is a mutable sign (as are Virgo, Sagittarius, and Pisces), which means it doesn't initiate with its energy like a cardinal sign (Aries, Cancer, Libra, Capricorn) and doesn't hold on to its element like fixed signs (Taurus, Leo, Scorpio, Aquarius). This means they are riding the waves of their intellectual curiosity. When you think of the element of Air, think about libraries, YouTube video essays, Wikipedia, documentaries, gossip from a subway, and school lectures. Air is all about intellect, communication, cognition, and reason, whether formal or informal. It's an element that doesn't fuck around with emotions (Water), ideals (Fire), or the material (Earth). It likes to cut through all the B.S. of the world with stone-cold logic. So basically, when we think of Gemini, we think of a sign that's all about talking shit, learning all it can, and circulating that information as much as possible.

As the third sign of the zodiac, Gemini's journey starts with an understanding that there is much to focus on in this world besides yourself. They start asking questions about the world. They want to know as much as they can about it. For what reason? No one can be too sure. But they do seem to think that storing and knowing so much information will eventually lead them to some kind of universal truth. But is that ever the case? Does anyone ever find out the secret of the universe? It may remain a mystery to most people, but the central element of a Gemini's life lies in trying to find out.

Gemini is ruled by Mercury, the "divine trickster," the Greek god of wisdom, literature, travel, jokers, thieves, messages, and transitions. Mercury is a divine being seeking knowledge just for the sake of knowing things. He also enjoys testing people's intelligence; breaking apart and picking at concepts, words, and truths; pushing words to their absolute extreme and playing with them; and showing the blind side of people's thinking. Gemini represents the trickster side of Mercury, while its more serious counterpart, Virgo, represents the deity's healer side. So, like Mercury descended to Earth, Gemini is a brilliant debater with an encyclopedic (though perhaps superficial) knowledge of history and politics, but Gemini is also the most likely sign to believe they're better and smarter than everyone around them. On your first date, you'll be charmed by a Gemini, and on the second, you'll realize you can't stand them—or worse, you'll fall hard and be absolutely ruined by this charming and sometimes careless sign.

Geminis are guided by love: love for books, knowledge, thrills, and the unknown. Getting their attention doesn't take much. Geminis will talk to anyone—they are not known to be discerning when it comes to being curious about others. So seize the opportunity and attempt to keep them chatting. If you can hold a conversation, you've got them: the ability to banter is all they really look for in a partner. If you can keep up with the chatter for hours on end, they will fall for you. It's just that easy! However, keeping them committed is a trickier affair.

The shadow side of Gemini's brilliance and curiosity about the world is that they often become detached, almost as if they aren't a part of it. If you want to get a better understanding of Gemini, consider the myth of Castor and Pollux. As the myth goes, these twins were born half brothers, hatched from an egg. One twin's father was the all-mighty god Zeus, and the other twin just had a human king as a father. These two children became warriors and were inseparable. Unfortunately, one of them was not immortal. When the mortal brother died, the other brother cried and begged Zeus to bring him back. Zeus answered the call and made a deal with them: they could both live, but every year they would have to switch places. One would live with the gods on Olympus while the other would spend time on Earth as a mortal.

The myth of the twins shows us that Gemini has a natural talent for being able to see and experience life in more than one dimension. Gemini has a natural connection to the divine realm. You can always catch a Gemini by the way they look at you. These people, always in the act of doing a million things, never really slow down; but when they see you, they see *through* you. When a Gemini stares at you, they're analyzing your psychic framework and your way of being, not just looking at your butt (but possibly also looking at your butt).

These people are living not just in this reality but on a mercurial plane as well. And you can be damn sure that a Gemini is trying to find stimulation and meaning in every interaction they have in their everyday life. Since Gemini is often neutral in their opinions and morality, people like to go to them to vent and share their secrets. But while Gemini may be a good listener, their record for keeping the goods private is spotty. Geminis love to gossip, and sometimes they keep sensitive information to themselves, but they will share information if it becomes too much for them to sit on in isolation. I tell Geminis they might want to consider having an "alt" account on their social media platform, an alternate profile where they can rant and disseminate information to work things out instead of indiscriminately blowing up people's lives when the burden of knowing something juicy is just too much to bear. Gemini understands the black, white, and gray of the world. They don't discriminate when acquiring knowledge or people—they're just hungry for knowledge and experience and are primarily interested in acquiring new subjects that can get them closer to the "why" of it all.

Gemini is happy when they're in motion. They can't remain still for too long. They can't be stuck with the same people for too long. They need gossip, new information, or life will no longer feel exciting. So don't rely on Gemini if you're looking for loyalty. Gemini will text you ferociously and constantly for forty-eight hours, and then you'll never hear from them again. Gemini will make you feel like you're the most important person in the room, and the next time you see them, they'll walk right past you as if you were a stranger. Gemini is fascinating, magnetic, charming—but can be a total dick.

For example, Gemini is known for being two-faced. This often happens to be true, because they can't seem to keep their mouths closed. For them, there's no kind of knowledge that should be kept from public consumption, no matter how dark or precious. There isn't an NDA in the world that can keep a Gemini's mouth shut. So don't give your heart to them or let them in on your deepest truth—unless you want it to be the basis of their next novel, a post on social media, or just so widely known that you'll hear about it from the guy at the deli downstairs.

As the first mutable sign, Gemini knows all about code-switching. Code-switching is a term I learned long ago from one of my friends, and in general from growing up as a person of color. When we go from place to place, from our parents to our friend groups, we pick up and adapt our personality to fit those social environments. And as Gemini is all about seeking knowledge, of course they will adapt and learn the language in an instant. Sure, they may not stay consistent in their personality or mannerisms—they'll instantly adapt to whatever situation they're in. But really, who is the same person with everyone? Our mother will never know us the way our friends do, our lover will never understand how our father sees us, our enemies will never understand why our best friend feels so connected to us.

In astrology, there is a term called *esoteric ruler*. We can think of it as the north compass of our sign, its inner truth. Venus is the esoteric ruler of Gemini, so we can infer that—through all the knowledge-seeking and hyperactive investigation of people, places, things, and ideas—Gemini is really just trying to find love. They are trying to find all the right pieces of information that will bring people together, help us all understand one another better, improve people's way of being, and better understand the meaning of existence. This is to say that, even if you want to kill the Gemini in your life for being impossible to pin down socially, a mile-a-minute talker who is also an insufferable know-it-all, remember that Gemini's ultimate goal is connection. Maybe that will keep you from launching them into space the next time they share your secrets at a dinner party, take an hour deciding where to eat dinner, leave you at a party when they find a shiny rock on the floor, or change their tone of voice and identity when they're in a new environment.

CANCER SUN

JUNE 21– JULY 22

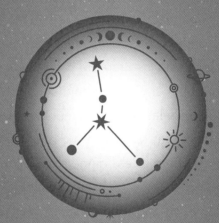

ARCHETYPE: The caregiver, the mom friend, the stage 4 clinger

MODALITY: Cardinal

ELEMENT: Water

HOUSE: 4th (home, private life, nurturing, family, roots, childhood)

ANATOMY: Chest, stomach

RULER: Moon

ESOTERIC RULER: Neptune

QUOTE: "I made you some cookies and liked all your posts back to 2004. Are we best friends now?"

s Gemini season ends, we reach the final chapter of the zodiac story, which is also a story about the self. In Aries, we learn how to grab hold of our identity; in Taurus, we learn about our values; and in Gemini, we learn to communicate and interact with the world. Once we get to Cancer, the sun sets and we are asked to come back home. Primordial feelings arise as we watch the sun set, say goodbye to the day, and experience a deep longing never felt before. We wonder what all these feelings are about. We wonder where these feelings of joy and sadness come from, and why it feels like we're the only one in the world who has ever experienced any of these things.

Cancer is the first Water sign of the zodiac. Water signs are all about emotions, and, as the first of the three Water signs, Cancer's understanding of emotions isn't all that deep. When Cancer freaks out about something, or is touched by something that moves them, they tend to think they're the first human who has ever felt or experienced emotions, and you can't tell them differently. It's not like you can tell a Cancer that their emotions are nothing special. They think what they're going through is a once-in-a-lifetime, unique experience.

These people live and react based on their emotions. Instinctually, they can be very psychic: if you catch a Cancer talking to themselves, listen closely, because they might be predicting something big that's yet to come. Perhaps their best quality is that they can pick up on the psychic current of everything going on around them. However, these people have a hard time explaining what exactly it is that they are talking about. Perhaps this is to compensate for thinking too much about emotions and things beyond this plane of reality. Perhaps it is just because Cancer lives in a different world themselves.

As a sign traditionally ruled by the Moon, the sign of the mother, Cancers have a strong relationship with family. Cancer Suns are known for being protective of those they care about. They can also be overbearing and clingy to those they form an immediate, close bond with. They are a cardinal sign, after all, so when they feel something, they go straight into action. Just try to tell a Cancer to slow their roll and calm down—it isn't going to happen, even if it's obvious that their impulsive actions are going to absolutely ruin your life. It isn't until we get to Scorpio that we find a Water sign that is actually careful about how they use other people's emotions.

Cancer Suns live their truth by acting and initiating life through their emotions, no matter how superficial they may be. So, basically, it's an exhausting existence. When your truth is guided by a planet all about responding to your emotions, it's no wonder lots of Cancers just tend to stay at home. The world can test them every second, and these sensitive flowers feel that threat every minute they spend outside the walls of their homes. If they were to look at their polar opposite sign, Capricorn, they would learn that they need to set up boundaries. But Cancers usually don't get that far.

A Cancer Sun will often spend their life reacting and figuring out how to channel the power of their emotions, building and growing their emotional walls so they can better use their sensitive nature to benefit themselves and the lives of the people around them. Since Cancer is a cardinal sign, they have a lot of motivation to do something with their emotions. However, they can get caught up in petty emotions, easy highs, and insecurities.

As a sign of great maternal instinct, Cancer is one you can be sure you'll be safe around. These people aren't afraid to fight the bosses of the world, the kings of the world, the billionaires. In astrology, we find Jupiter to be exalted in Cancer. Jupiter is the planet of expansion and luck and bestows the energy of a great parent. Cancer, accordingly, is the #1 mom or #1 dad, wanting nothing more than to keep on giving all they can for their children to be the best they can be. Jupiter, a planet that knows nothing about boundaries, loves them for that. Cancer, although the most emotionally immature sign in the zodiac, has so much to give and so much to fight for. Their journey in life is to figure out how to build a home, nurture their environment, and secure their home.

If you follow a Cancer on social media, you'll notice they make it a habit to tell the world what they are into and are all about divulging their favorite vices. If they are a little more secretive, then just look at the celebrities/influencers they follow for clues. For example, if they like food accounts, take them to trendy restaurants. If they are really into musicians, go to a record store for their favorite bands on vinyl or plan to dance somewhere that plays their favorite type of music. If they like drinking, then take them out to a really fun bar. If all else fails, make them food. Cancers are suckers for a sweet treat.

LEO SUN

JULY 23–AUGUST 22

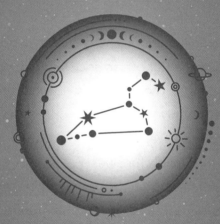

ARCHETYPE: The king, the theater kid, the guy who takes karaoke way too seriously

. . . .

MODALITY: Fixed

. . . .

ELEMENT: Fire

. . . .

HOUSE: 5th (romance, dating, hobbies, the inner child, risk-taking, creation, children, and just plain fun)

. . . .

ANATOMY: Heart, spine

. . . .

RULER: Sun

. . . .

ESOTERIC RULER: Sun

. . . .

QUOTE: "Stand back, it's Celine Dion time."

o one makes the summers hotter, the winters colder, the forest greener, or a love hotter than a Leo. Think of a bonfire: it's the center of attention, you let it keep you warm on cold nights, its light drives away the dark, and its flames can swallow up sad memories. The energy of Cancer is crying under the night skies, processing emotions, and taking care of the home and family. When we finally get to Leo, our energy turns to having fun: we go out to enjoy our time in the sun, we fuck around, set up pranks, get blackout drunk at concerts, find romance for the night, and dive into every hedonistic urge. Leo is a fixed Fire sign, and like all fixed signs, they are the embodiment of their element. Fire is an element all about spirit, inspiration, hope, faith, and—although most astrologers debate this—love.

Chocolate, wine, and mimosas, Leo is the epitome of glamour and life. They like to engage with the public, spend hours researching what's cool right now, love talking to strangers and asking them about their opinions on the current climate. Just like Aries, they do tend to talk about themselves a lot! However, unlike Aries, Leo is always trying to take the public's temperature, see what people are listening to, investigate where people are getting their clothes, and examine the problems everyone else is facing. The last thing a Leo wants to be seen as is ignorant or stupid. In the end, they do a lot of talking, if only so they can get a better sense of what they actually—or at least *should*—care about in this world.

As your resident Leo Sun, the person who's writing this book, I do have to say that Leos have an ego problem. If you insult them, they will dedicate themselves to making a whole tweet/post about you—although they would never directly call you out or mention you by name, because that shit is undignified. Being a victim is a Cancer quality, so instead of licking their wounds and eliciting pity, Leo will just draw out the drama to be bigger and more cinematic than it probably is. Leos are prideful—they have fights with gods, not humans. If you believe in esoteric astrology, then you must know that before coming into this existence, Leo spent their past lives mastering their own emotions. They understand how undignified, petty, fleeting, superficial, and exhausting it is to let your emotions control you. Leos understand emotions clearly, and they understand how to set up boundaries. And in this existence, they understand that heroes don't go around moping. Lions don't cry, they pick themselves right up and get right to business.

Often the general understanding of ego calls to mind celebrity culture and self-obsessed influencers: ego is seen as nothing more than a toxic narcissism. Those who are slaves to ego only care about themselves, destroy others who wound their pride, and always seem to be getting caught up in a grand drama of their own design. Leos get a bad reputation for being egomaniacs of this sort, tied up in their obsession with their self-image, wanting to be adored by the crowd; but if they're guilty of anything, it is their harmless vanity. Narcissism is something rooted in deep hatred and self-loathing. But Leos understand how important the self is, and they do what they can so they can love and improve themselves. They want to radiate and shine their light to the world.

One thing you must remember about Leo is that it's one of four signs (Virgo, Libra, Scorpio) that are known for being social. Leo is someone who takes all their accumulated knowledge about feelings, values, and communication and puts it toward the cultivation of a self-image. Leo's existence is all about using this wisdom to understand themselves and share the wisdom with the world.

They seek for others to understand passion, to love themselves, to light up the world through their ideals.

Gold and radiant, Leo's love is something so fiery and cinematic that it can rival your most romantic Hollywood movie. To get the love of these lions, you must not be afraid to audition and screen-test for the leading role in the movie that is their lives. Leos are naturally drawn to people who place them firmly in the spotlight. So keep complimenting them and don't hold back. Leos love a corny pickup line as much as they like eating up compliments. Continuously flattering and complimenting them will always catch their attention—don't be afraid to exaggerate. Like their domesticated feline kin, Leos like to play with their food. They will poke into your life, they will ask about the most intimate details of your world, and then they will wait until the passion is too much to pour their heart out. It's a long game. If a Leo comes after you, chances are you won't see it coming. They are naturally so bright and bubbly, their flirtatious nature can fly under the radar. But Leos are generous above all and like to shine the spotlight on others as much as they like having it on themselves. If you're big and bold enough to catch a Leo's notice, you might find yourself (at least momentarily) the star of the show.

VIRGO SUN

AUGUST 23–SEPTEMBER 22

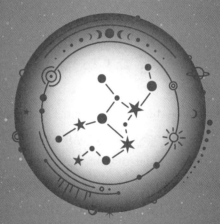

ARCHETYPE: The healer, the copy editor, the solution to a problem you didn't want solved

MODALITY: Mutable

ELEMENT: Earth

HOUSE: 6th (health and wellness, diet, detoxes, physical limitations)

ANATOMY: Lungs, nervous system

RULER: Mercury

ESOTERIC RULER: Moon

QUOTE: "I've analyzed your every flaw; please love me."

I t is your birthday. You throw a party, keep your guests drunk, and are the star of the show— everyone feeds off your energy. Then the sun comes up, the party has to end, people leave, and the only person picking up the pieces of the shattered disco ball is you. The fun and celebration are over and you know you have to fix your mess. You are a Virgo Sun: the most anal-retentive, nitpicky, critical, analytical, neurotic, and freaky sign of the zodiac. You would think a mutable sign would be easygoing, adaptable, and open-minded. However, Virgo is full of constant critique, a voice in their head making commentary about everything, worrying forever about the minuscule details of everyday life. However, it's important to remember that with every critique and comment Virgo makes, they are trying to find ways to make life better. In the journey through the zodiac, we find the energy of the healer in this sign. Healers want to be of service to others, no matter how much they fight their own egos to surrender to those needs. Virgo is that to a tee: they're incredibly annoying and just won't get off your back about this or that. But at heart, they just want you to be happy.

Ruled by Mercury, Virgo shares its ruler with Gemini. Gemini is happy learning just for the sake of learning. Virgo, on the other hand, is more meticulous in terms of the information they absorb. Gemini loves to gossip, share secrets, and ask for advice in order to gain a better perception of what is expected of them. Virgo isn't much of a gossip. Virgo is an Earth sign, so they have mastered the self; they look at the reality of what's in front of them to make the most out of it. While Gemini uses information to help themselves, Virgo doesn't care about information unless it can improve and heal whatever it is they're going to start talking shit about.

Virgo loves to call people out. They notice the tiniest bit of hypocrisy, count their pennies, double-check the stove, and keep score of what's due to them. Pay their Venmo requests, or they will hunt you down. Virgo is the biggest perfectionist in the zodiac and can't understand why everyone isn't the same. These people go into any room and immediately start surveying their environment. They are constantly organizing their own bookshelves and will get to work on yours if you give them even the slightest hint that you'd appreciate it. They deep-clean their homes often; and if there's anything they love, it's dusting thoroughly and dousing everything in bleach. They are analytical about everything, from their appearance to the color of the sky to the punctuation of their lover's text messages. They use periods at the end of their own texts, and it's really hard to tell whether their messages are meant to be threatening or just grammatically correct.

Virgo is very much aware of how important words and information are, and they have the gift of knowing when some information is just not worth chasing after. Unless their other placements say otherwise, they won't be caught gossiping with neighbors just to shoot the shit, and they won't ask you about your feelings until you come up to them and ask to talk.

When it comes to a relationship, Virgo Sun tends to seek either someone they can fix or someone who can help them escape reality. Perhaps both? Virgos do love a little renovation, someone they can make feel safe and sound. They like to fix people and the environment. Giving yourself over to others in the service of fixing them does seem to be virtuous in some sense; but in another sense, it is very stupid. Virgos can get blinded by the potential in anyone and not know when to give up. They can get so caught up in the most superficial aspects of their renovation projects that they can't see the big picture. This goes not only for relationships but also for life. If they forgot to mop, if they didn't wash the dishes, if they didn't go for a run—would any of it matter in the larger scheme of life?

Cool, analytical, and calculating, Virgo is one of those zodiac signs so emotionally distant and in their head, it almost seems impossible to get their romantic attention. Their expectations are high. They can't help but try to find flaws and criticize everything, including their own romantic taste and emotions. Even when they don't know exactly what they want in a romantic partner, they try to intellectualize their desires. Ruled by Mercury, Virgos tend to be very nervous and to overanalyze why they feel the way they do whenever someone pulls on their heartstrings. The way to their heart is through communication, building trust over time, and by being patient with them. If a Virgo is after you, they will try to analyze and learn everything about you. They like to be useful and will offer themselves in service to those they like. They are also very critical of how you treat others, so be sure to have manners with everyone you come across when you are in front of them. Rude to the waiter? You will be rejected. They have a soft spot for people in the service industry, pets, nurses, and those who make it a career to help others. To catch a Virgo's attention, it's important to be straightforward, be confident, be yourself.

Virgo's esoteric ruler is the Moon, the cosmic nurturer, our eternal mother. Virgo finds a purpose in being Captain Save-a-Ho. After all, in the zodiac, someone has to be a savior. There are not that many of them out there—but many are Virgos. Yet, despite their anal retention and tight-end attitude, Virgos love to get down and be freaky. When it comes to sex, Virgos consider it a recreational hobby, although also an activity with a higher purpose. They want to have fun, but they also want to ascend. They want to connect with something more spiritual out there. They are more likely to have a weed dependency than any other zodiac sign, and it makes a lot of sense for them. When you are constantly worried about what's going on here on earth, you can lose your head rather quickly when things don't go according to plan. So, for a sign under such intense pressure, it makes sense that activities that release and calm are attractive.

Basically, if you want to catch a Virgo's attention, pretend to be helpless. And if you want them to help you, all you have to do is ask directly, to their face. They will be all over you. If you want to know who's going to double-check your pronunciation, call a Virgo. If you want someone to run a background check on a potential date, call a Virgo. These people, as attentive and neurotic as they are, will always make room to heal and care for others. When we get to Virgo, we get a sign that, when balanced, has mastered the self in conjunction with others. They are always looking to find ways to help others through their actions, which, even when mundane, can be quite important. Through Virgo, we understand the meaning of rituals. Virgo is all about working every day in the service of grander things. In Virgo, we learn that taking care of others and ourselves fills life with more beautiful meaning and connection. If only Virgo would just get off our backs and stop complaining about the typos in our texts.

LIBRA SUN

SEPTEMBER 23–OCTOBER 22

ARCHETYPE: The diplomat, the sophisticate, the supreme lord of superficiality

ELEMENT: Air

MODALITY: Cardinal

HOUSE: 7th (best friends, business partners, lovers, enemies, mirrors, contracts)

ANATOMY: Heart, spine, kidneys

RULER: Venus

ESOTERIC RULER: Uranus

QUOTE: "I'm *such* a Libra."

ouldn't it be nice to sleep around and never catch feelings? Wouldn't it be nice if you didn't have to step over people to get what you want? Wouldn't it be nice if you could solve every centuries-old feud between nations? Wouldn't it be nice to stand in everyone's good graces when you are asked to show your allegiance? Wouldn't it be great if life were black and white, and the right answer were so obvious?

Libra, the scales. The sign of adjustment, the only sign in the zodiac that is not represented by anything from the natural world, which is fitting for their personality. Libra is the zodiac sign that is trying to relate. Trying to find a way to make peace with their biggest enemy. Libra is an activist. Libra wants to be on everyone's good side. They stand for ideals, but they also take into consideration the ideals of others.

In Aries, we find the individual, the sign opposite Libra (and therefore representative of Libra's shadow side), where we find an archetype trying to extend themselves and connect with others. If you think of the zodiac as a story, in Libra we are finally confronted by the "other." Libra is no longer working for others to find their own truth, like Virgo. Libra is not trying to find their talent and shine among the people, like Leo. Libra is seeing all the chaos and fighting that is caused by everyone's own individuality. Libra knows too well that we can't all have it our own way, as much as we would want to. Libra is the first to cut through people's individual bullshit and try to find a common ground.

Perfume-scented letters, casual shade, sweet talks, poetic vagueness, and white lies. Sun in Libra, just like any Libra placement, adds a level of elegance. Libra knows all the romantic movie tropes to make anyone fall for them. They know how to talk their way out of anything and circle around a topic endlessly (depending on what they feel is needed). Their specialty, more than anything else, is small talk—so the rest of us all kind of hate them. Leos and other Libras are probably the only people who find them special. Leos chat with others to make a memorable impression. Libras use small talk to find a way to make a connection. Small talk for them is reconnaissance to figure out how to gain an advantage. That's why Libras are the social climbers of the zodiac.

Creators of romance and poetic prose, Libras are also the most lovesick sign of the zodiac. As a reminder, they are a sign that is all about personal relationships and finding balance with others. With the ruler of Libra being Venus, it is a sign that is about the elevation of worldly values. As an Air sign, Libra values communication, thoughts, arts, music, connection, and aesthetics. Libra tries to see the beauty in people and is considered a social sign that tries to be around others just so they can pick apart parts of someone's personality so that they can adopt them as their own. Mirroring someone's mannerisms and personality is one of the most telltale signs that a Libra is into you and is a way to get into their heart. They like to see the best of themselves in others. They like being around other people who also value how they look and their taste in things. This may seem superficial, but Libra cares about beauty and someone's value. They can tell a lot about someone and the types of things they value based on the way they dress and care for themselves. If you ever try to get with a Libra, brush up on your aesthetics, prepare a personal candlelight dinner, and serenade them. As long as it fits their aesthetic, nothing is too much: a bed of roses, a velvet box filled with diamonds, caviar, whatever.

But it's not all completely superficial for this sign. Libras are always trying to figure out some big spiritual truth about themselves. They're looking for meaning. They are constantly reading poetry, watching movies, engaging with others: all of it is to better understand their own psychic woes. They want to have a solid emotional ground comprised of layers of meaning that explain why they love the things they love. If you spend a lot of time thinking about yourself, you're gonna come out of it being a good medium for ghosts. I have a theory that Libras make the best mediums and great psychologists. Either way, they know how to sweet-talk any demon.

SCORPIO SUN

OCTOBER 23–NOVEMBER 21

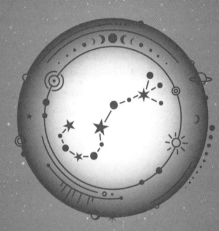

ARCHETYPE: The alchemist, the ultimate edgelord, the vampire sparkle prince

MODALITY: Fixed

ELEMENT: Water

HOUSE: 8th (secrets, psychology, death, rebirth, other people's money, survival, the occult)

ANATOMY: Blood, bowels, nose

RULER: Mars, Pluto

ESOTERIC RULER: Mars

QUOTE: "I am the darkness that creeps across the land; also, where is your bathroom?"

ex addicts, riptides, dark wizards, psychic vampires, Death cards, and the macabre: that's Scorpio, a Satanic holiday present all tied up with a neat little bow. If Cancer is the surface of the ocean where life flourishes and the water is clear, Scorpio is the deep canyon at the bottom of the ocean. It is one of the most prominent examples of darkness, a place of mystery where no one can be sure how deep the water is, and there is no way of knowing what lies beneath it. Scorpio is the place most likely to be home to giant aquatic worms, sightless fish with jaws the size of Jeeps, and other mammoth and indescribable creatures that could wreak havoc on dry land. So while it's terrifying that all that is down there, at least it's tucked away from public sight.

Scorpio is a fixed Water sign, so it is a sign that holds on to all of its emotion closely. Scorpios understand how deep and destructive matters of the heart can be and resent themselves for having such strong feelings. And, wow, they have *very* strong feelings that could be destructive if unleashed. You can catch them writing breakup songs about a relationship they never had, stalking their middle school crushes long after they've grown up, and creating dummy accounts to keep tabs on people who have hurt them.

Scorpio is a sign of the extremes of desire. They are the opposite of Taurus: so where Taurus is constructing the scaffolding of their values and building on things that are tangible, Scorpio is pulling things apart. Scorpios understand that earthly desire is all but temporary and seek to build their lives on a foundation of passion. Forget stability: they'd rather burn up in the fires of their own obsessions. Scorpio doesn't just pursue a desire—they go a step above. They want to understand the deep-seated root of it all, the truth behind their emotions and motivations. They are, *uh*, intense.

Ruled by Mars, the planet of war and passion, Scorpio tends to be aggressive, reactionary, and bold. Unlike Aries, they aren't hot-headed. Aries likes to strike while the iron is hot. Scorpio, on the other hand, likes to wait around until they can find their target's Achilles' heel. Aries goes for the beating; Scorpio goes for the kill. Scorpio is subtle and withdrawn compared to Aries. Scorpio describes the premeditated thoughts that lead to the actions we take. Scorpio is ruled by the planet Pluto. It makes sense: Pluto is all about the occult, survival, extremes, and all things goth. However, the energy of Pluto is a kind of extreme that many of us don't truly get to witness. Pluto is an atomic bomb, showing us the worst of what humans are capable of doing to destroy one another in the midst of war.

Associated with taxes, rebirth, death, hauntology—the things that keep people up at night—Scorpio goes deeper than many of the signs before them. In their quest for wholeness, they are not looking to prove themselves or understand themselves. They are very much aware of who they are. Their quest is to face the darker aspects of their personality so they can push forward even more. Are you goth as hell? If you're a Scorpio, your life's journey will be to get even gothier. And woe betide anyone who stands in their way. They are very ambitious people who are willing to go to the ends of the earth to fulfill their desires.

In astrology, where you find Scorpio in a chart is the place you feel a need to be secretive and intense. Those who have their Sun in Scorpio are inherently suspicious of others and, as such, rarely show others who they really are. They are the kind of people who will go out of their way to avoid revealing their middle names, the number of people in their family, their schedule, their age—whatever. It's not just that they think you'll try to hack into their bank account. There is just always something they try to keep hidden from the world, perhaps for shits and giggles, perhaps for some more overarching reason. Some people say that where there's Scorpio in a chart, there is something about that person that will always be hidden from the eyes of the world. And though, as mentioned, this tendency is quite reflexive, at heart it mostly comes from a fear of being powerless. When you refuse to divulge, or even articulate, every detail about yourself, you retain a certain kind of leverage. Scorpio is that mystery—where a person finds feeling so deep and intense that it is beyond words or even conscious integration into the self. When you give yourself endless freedom to be who you are without having to share it with the world, your abilities are limitless. Of course, it really sucks if you're trying to make idle conversation, and first dates tend to be either earth-shattering or very, very frustrating.

For Scorpio, most of their sense of self will come from mastering their ego. Understanding their desires. Being open to change. Having the endurance to let go of habits that keep them from evolving and to let go of hurt in their hearts. It's not surprising that Scorpio has a reputation for being scary and dark, because if we held on to pain for as long as they do, we'd be faced with the same risk: that tendency, when left to perpetuate itself unchecked, will turn anyone into either a loner or a villain. Scorpio is the dark night of the zodiac, where the individual goes to face their demons and come out a changed and more improved person. Or they turn into Batman, who is generally a huge downer at parties.

Among all the signs, no one longs for romance so intensely and passionately as a Scorpio. They see right through people and are very cool with staring deep into the abyss if it means a soul-deep connection. Because when it comes to romance and the pursuit of love, everything is life or death for Scorpio. They can't have half-assed feelings; they won't pursue anyone romantically if it doesn't make their blood boil with intensity. They want passion, their heart to be racing, a soul-bonding love. If you ever find yourself falling for a Scorpio, be as direct as possible and unleash all the emotions and passion you can hold in your heart. Scorpio wants to feel like they're letting go of all the emotions that they can possibly muster without any judgment—that's the epitome of love for them. So, basically, they're teen-vampire-novel protagonists come to life. If that gets you going, definitely go for a Scorpio.

SAGITTARIUS SUN

NOVEMBER 22–DECEMBER 21

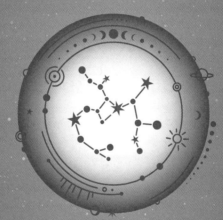

ARCHETYPE: The adventurer, the girl who studied abroad in France and never stops talking about it

ELEMENT: Fire

MODALITY: Mutable

HOUSE: 9th (higher thinking, travel, philosophy, religion, publishing, foreign countries, lawyers, faith)

ANATOMY: Hips

RULER: Jupiter

ESOTERIC RULER: Earth

QUOTE: "Once you have Cantal in Lyon, you'll never be able to go back to American cheese."

ay goodbye to your goth days, bid farewell to the gates of hell, and stop mourning your old self. It's time to talk about the fiery Sagittarius. Sagittarius is the sign of the philosopher, the adventurer, the know-it-all, the loudmouth, and the optimist. There's some good stuff in there and some irritating stuff, so let's dig in. Sagittarius is the last of the three Fire signs: Aries represents the spark, Leo represents the core of the resulting flame, and Sagittarius represents its dancing tendrils as it grows. You can put your hands over the flame and it will keep you warm. Sagittarius is the fire that inspires and spreads warmth to all those who gather around it. Just be aware that a sudden gust can set off the burning of a village. Any challenge to their individuality can set them off and ignite a war. Yet they are equally likely to use that fire to defend the rights of others: they are the first to advocate for anyone who would dare belittle someone's heart. So, yes, they are amazing hosts, making their friends feel full of warm, fuzzy feelings . . . as long as those friends never say the wrong thing. Then they're fucked for life!

Sagittarius, being ruled by Jupiter, is a sign of extravagance. Jupiter is a planet all about expanding boundaries. In Sagittarius, it lends itself to seeking out new experiences, new cultures, new languages, new inspiration. Sagittarius tends to be very giving, very optimistic, and (at least in ideal conditions) very easy-going and open to whatever life has to offer. However, because the influence of Jupiter is constantly prompting Sagittarius to expand their boundaries, people with their Sun in this sign don't stick with anything for too long. They view life as an expedition, so nothing could possibly be more important than their search for the universal truth at the journey's end. Not Mom, not Dad, not their soulmate, not their dog. (Sorry, dog!) Don't expect Sagittarius to bow to sentimentality, moral duty, or any of the other stuff that might make most other people stay the course. And don't expect them to be satisfied with one party when there might be something better happening! More than any other sign, they suffer from severe FOMO. They always think the grass is greener on the other side. Like Scorpio, Sagittarius is dedicated to turning over every stone in search of the truth; but unlike Scorpio, darkness doesn't interest them much if it can't provide inspiration for growth. So Sagittarius is less inclined toward the gothy darkness of the soul and might be more into Buddhist sutras, green architecture, Derrida, or acid jazz. Whatever inspires them. But never for too long.

Straightforward as they come, the symbol of Sagittarius is that of an arrow. These people are blunt and direct. They get straight to the point, even if you'd rather they didn't. And diplomacy? Forget it. There are truths to be uncovered! Being nice is definitely not something they prioritize. It's just that Sagittarius has a fundamental inability to mess around with any small talk or to play games with people. If someone or something makes them uncomfortable, they will address it. And their words can (and do!) pierce the hearts of those who are sensitive. Sagittarius has a reputation for being cruel because they tend to be truthful for truth's sake and don't think too hard about whether they're shattering anyone's fragile little heart.

Sagittarius is a sign of abundance, and they tend to have a lot of friends. However, they also tend to only share their secrets with a select few. One thing to note with Sagittarius is that they like to accept every invitation that gets handed to them. They are generous to everyone, even if that means being quadruple-booked.

They're supposed to be the maid of honor at your wedding, but someone invited them to an aerial yoga class? Sorry, bride! Sagittarius only sticks around with people who are accepting of both their boundless wisdom (and/or inability to accept their lack of it) and their need to be free (or alternately, their impersonal but inevitable need to ditch you if something more interesting comes along).

Free and wild, Sagittarius will always be found galloping around drunk on the fumes from the highs and lows of their latest adventure. Ruled by a mutable and passionate element, these people live for spontaneity and wanderlust. They get turned off by clingy people, and they take time to form lasting relationships. They don't do well when they are tied up, but they do view romance as an appealing experience. It's just that they want the whole package, and they are often notorious for jumping in and out of relationships as quickly as it takes to walk from Times Square to Grand Central (for readers not familiar with New York geography, that's about four crosstown blocks, or ten, maybe fifteen minutes). Sagittarians are not known to be picky when it comes to their relationships and romantic pursuits. They'll often seek out those who come from a foreign place or have at least lived a life foreign to the one they live. Fun accents are practically irresistible for the well-traveled Sagittarius—their provenance doesn't even really matter that much.

Sagittarians do make their interest known right away with blunt flirtation and obvious romantic gestures. Subtlety's not really their forte or interest; you can easily spot them winking with cartoonish intensity, repeatedly calling you cute, and talking to everyone they meet about how much they'd like to bone you. So that part is not hard. Winning their heart, though? Trickier. The only person who can truly light a Sagittarian's heart on fire is someone who can keep them excited and talking for hours on end. If you want to pursue them, though, be cautious, because these people aren't known to settle down for too long. They have such a rich inner philosophy that they often can't help leaving to chase the grass on the other side (they've heard it's greener, so—sorry!).

Sagittarius believes in the law of abundance. They try to treat everyone fairly. They hate gatekeepers, critical people who lack a sense of humor, and buzzkills of all sorts. They think life has no limits and that there is enough to go around for everyone, and therefore no one should ever tell them no. They want to bring joy and wisdom to the whole earth with no obstacles and view themselves as multidimensional bringers of truth and happiness. However, because they do tend to overextend themselves, they're very likely to burn out when things get to be too much. They detach, they dis-engage, and then they head off somewhere more free without bothering to wrap up loose ends. Screw the haters! Off to more enlightened pastures. Sorry about your wedding, I guess.

In the end, Sagittarius has much to learn about what it truly means to be giving and free. After the darkness of Scorpio, Sagittarius emerges to find higher truth. Sagittarius wants to correct the world and do what they can to restore order and find justice. The Libra interpre-tation of justice is fairness, negotiation, and meeting people where they are. Sagittarius, however, believes they know what's best, and they aren't afraid to execute a decision. Is that decision sometimes catastrophically wrong? Yes, absolutely. But it will definitely be made quickly and decisively, so at least there's that?

CAPRICORN SUN

DECEMBER 22–JANUARY 19

ARCHETYPE: The father, the final boss, the actual boss who seems to have no beating human heart

MODALITY: Cardinal

ELEMENT: Earth

HOUSE: 10th (career, reputation, authority figures, responsibility, higher self)

ANATOMY: Knees

RULER: Saturn

ESOTERIC RULER: Saturn

QUOTE: "Laddering ETFs is the most reliable method of long-term investment."

In the video game that is the zodiac, Capricorn is the final boss of not only the Earth signs, but the entire zodiac. The most mature of the Earth signs, as well as the last of the cardinal signs, Capricorn can be pretty intimidating, even though they are also often boring, pedantic, and money-hungry. They'll step over the wounded bodies of their friends in pursuit of the last sale-priced bag of chips. That said, they wield amazing power that can be used for good if it isn't wasted on achieving material success.

If we look at the zodiac as a story, Sagittarius is when someone goes off to college or on a faraway trip. They acquire new knowledge and expand their belief systems, finding passion beyond what's been possible. They take a class and recognize systemic issues that have held society back for generations, and they begin to want to do more than the people who came before them. They don't want to end up like Mom and Dad— they want to ascend to a higher level of consciousness! In Capricorn, a universal sign, they've come to an elevated understanding of themselves, their beliefs, and the ways of other people. Unlike Sagittarius, Capricorns aren't college kids who went to France and feel like they really *get* art, *Mom*. Capricorns are past that: they're trying to climb their way through the ranks so they can take charge of this planet. Capricorn is an Earth sign, so they don't care too much about what's beyond their world. Elevated consciousness? It means nothing when you don't have cold, hard cash. Capricorns may seem like coldhearted bitches, but that's not quite their whole story (although it's totally part of their story!). Capricorn, after all, is represented by the mystical sea goat. The sea goat is half fish and half goat, so they understand emotions very well—it's just that they don't always care. They know what to leave behind so they can get that dollar when necessary.

In astrology, all the cardinal signs think they're the first to discover their element. Cardinal signs think that if everyone just knew what *they* knew, it would solve all the problems in this world. Aries thinks they're the first to discover belief and faith, so they go around telling people that if only they had faith in themselves, they could get shit done. Cancer thinks they're the first to discover emotions and intuition, so they go around telling others that if only they took action based on their gut feelings, life would work out for them. Libra believes that they're the first to ever have thoughts or use logic, so they go around telling people that if only they could think things through enough, life would unfold according to their wishes. As for Capricorn, they think they invented the grind. They're convinced that no one else knows that if they hustle enough, they'll get all they want out of life.

The other signs understand all these things (surprise, cardinal signs!). But fixed signs like to stay put, whereas mutable signs like to let go. Cardinal signs are all about motivating others: they believe they're here to lead the other signs into battle. Capricorn pushes themselves and others to keep going until their minds and bodies are weak. They don't acknowledge Watery emotions, Airy ethics, or Fiery ideals. As such, Capricorns get the reputation for being cold, work-oriented hard-asses. And it is not entirely unearned.

Capricorn is ruled by the planet Saturn and by Chronos, the god of time and karma. Saturn is all about restriction, responsibility, and hard work. If a planet is masked by Saturn, it tends to be characterized by both maturity and bitchiness. The people of Saturn have a killer resting bitch face. Unlike a Scorpio, who's trying to hide their emotions, or an Aquarius, who's trying to hide what they're thinking, a Capricorn remains reserved so as to compartmentalize in order to keep going at full speed. It's just when all those unfortunate thoughts and feelings hit them that things can get tricky.

Given that this sign is ruled by the god of time, it's not surprising that Capricorn is known to take their time and find love later in life. These people seek partners who are practical, persistent, and calm. Despite being known for having the emotional presence of a brick wall, Capricorns are actually very in touch with the inner workings of their heart. It's just that they're not super-interested in gushing or laying out their feelings in front of just anyone. When times are rough, Capricorn would rather stride through the day with an expression of calm disdain—then head home for a refreshing scream-cry.

So if you want to catch the romantic attention of a Capricorn, make sure to be at least half as cool as they are. Keep your shit together. Always present yourself at your most refined. Capricorn likes someone they can respect: patient and attentive, high-achieving, self-assured. And they're not in a hurry to connect with those who interest them. Capricorn could spend months (years!) learning about someone before they're ready to open up and be vulnerable. When it comes to romance, there isn't much—or any—strategy for these people. They want someone who comforts them, someone who reassures them. It's pretty simple. In that way, a Capricorn is an easy-to-figure-out beast. But their emotional lives have a dark side too.

Those with a Sun in Capricorn are in danger of being swallowed up by memories and melancholy when they least expect it. Their memories of where they came from tend to follow them around like ghosts. Capricorns often feel pressured to keep a legacy going, or their desire to work hard transforms without their knowledge into yet another way to get past the inconvenient emotions associated with their dark past. Capricorn is that coldhearted CEO whose commitment to work often masks a tragic backstory. Then again, Capricorn can just be your shitty manager, who's only not glum when he's putting together profit-and-loss statements and playing with pivot tables in Excel, or your soulless IRS auditor. As with all signs, its idiosyncrasies manifest in a variety of ways!

Money is an easy way for Capricorn to measure success, so therefore it is frequently their favorite. They tend not to care about Fiery spiritual enlightenment, Watery emotional comfort, or Airy humanitarian ideals. These people measure life by tangible results. Did you participate? Did you put in the hours? If you are dating them and you don't show proof that you are there for them and love them, they may just find someone who will take the time to show them the receipts. Like Libra, Capricorn can also be a social climber. Capricorn purposely does things to improve their appearance and place in the world, and they don't see anything wrong with that. While Libra might mask their intentions with small talk and good hair, Capricorn's methods are a little more unadorned. They're okay with asserting dominance and staring you down with dead eyes. They have no time for niceties and baldly want as much power as possible. So stay out of their way, and maybe you'll get a little touch of their sincerity, their earthy love, their steadfast loyalty. But just don't try to weigh them down.

AQUARIUS SUN

JANUARY 20–FEBRUARY 18

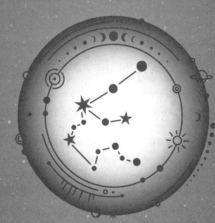

ARCHETYPE: The innovator, the revolutionary, the person who reposts PETA videos on a regular basis

MODALITY: Fixed

ELEMENT: Air

HOUSE: 11th (friendships, acquaintances, groups, hopes, dreams)

ANATOMY: Ankles (particularly the Achilles' heel), calves, shins, and the circulatory system

RULER: Saturn, Uranus

ESOTERIC RULER: Jupiter

QUOTE: "That sucks about your dog, but did you know that climate change causes 5 million deaths every year?"

hen you spend your days trying to rise to the top of the corporate ladder by building a legacy for yourself and trying to reign over the earth, the days tend to feel long, maybe agonizing. How many masters of the universe get near the summit, freak out, and quit to do something more meaningful? We are now talking about the Water Bearer, Aquarius. It is not a Water sign, despite the *aqua* in its name. In Aquarius, the corporate boss—perhaps after years of making assistants scramble for their coffee every morning—quits or retires from their job and tries to use all their earthly resources to help the needy. The Aquarius symbol is represented by someone who is pouring knowledge into the earth. As the most evolved of the Air signs, they aren't so much concerned about cultivating their personal ideals or even improving their ideals through their relationships; instead, they want to come up with concepts that will improve all of humanity. Which is probably why the Sun hates being in Aquarius. The Sun is all about the ego and being an individual. But how can you be an individual when you're thinking about the rest of the world? Well, thankfully we are in the twenty-first century, and maintaining communication with a large part of the population is a lot easier to do. We now have the Internet, which some occultists speculate is an Aquarian invention that connects us to societies all across the globe. And, though they are very much about ideals and logic that will help all of society, they tend to be aloof and forget about their mundane responsibilities on earth. For this reason, they very much aren't a Water sign. They're cool with helping the poor and starving, but it kind of sucks to work for them. And fall in love with an Aquarius? It's sometimes an exercise in masochism, even if you appreciate their lofty ideals. They won't comfort your emotions, because it's not helpful in the greater scheme of life—so if there is a cause to champion, get ready to suck it up.

For Aquarius, love is a best friend. They want someone they can invite to every party they are invited to, whose politics are similar to theirs, who is relatively liberal or independent (just like them). They like someone with their own personality, someone unique (kind of like them). So if you want to pursue an Aquarius, flatter them by taking them somewhere that reflects their own interests, particularly if it's an educational opportunity.

Take them to a museum or a science lab so they can exclaim about how much they like to learn. Accompany them to a film festival and then agree with their theories about visual narrative. Pick a protest you know they care about and invite them to paint a banner with you.

If there is one thing I can tell you about Aquarius, it's that they tend to have a superiority complex. They are the sign opposite Leo, which means that Leo is representative of their shadow qualities: while Leo's main-character complex is more harmless vanity and self-mythologization, Aquarius takes it an inch further and thinks they know better than anyone else in the world. An Aquarius feels they know you better than you know yourself. They are totally fine acting like the authority over people's thoughts and feelings.

Aquarius is ruled by Saturn and Uranus. Saturn's influence on Aquarius allows them to be stern and methodical, and to stubbornly fixate on their ideals. They tend to manifest into them, developing an air of superiority. Aquarians tend to have a capitalist mindset similar to that of Capricorn. But while Capricorn wants to see humans work themselves hard enough to achieve as much wealth and resources as they can on earth, Aquarius wants to see humanity be at their absolute best, achieve world peace, get rid of pollution, or whatever cause they decide to care about the most. Both these signs tend to loathe others for not being able to reach their highest levels of achievement. Capricorns despise laziness and people who don't work hard enough. Aquarians are repulsed by people for failing to improve in order to make the world a better place. As such, Aquarius tends to be the most aggressively woke, berating you with global/societal/ political issues in casual conversation, whether you like it or not. Sometimes Aquarius does have a point: why cry about the guy who ghosted you, when the world is burning and children are getting bombed? Aquarius is here to think about the big picture and could care less about issues that don't affect the world at large. And maybe you can't count on an Aquarius to sit down and comfort you, but at least Aquarius is working on a cure for cancer, a solution to world hunger, or whatever other improvements will save our society. Or destroy us all. Whatever Aquarius deems most important!

PISCES SUN

FEBRUARY 19–MARCH 20

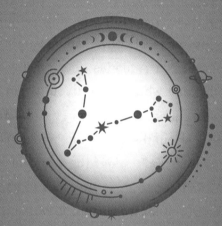

ARCHETYPE: The dreamer, the fan-fiction writer, the friendly binge-drinker

MODALITY: Mutable

ELEMENT: Water

HOUSE: 12th (hidden enemies, endings, past lives, blind spots, prison, things that can hold you hostage, the unconscious, escapism)

ANATOMY: Feet

RULER: Neptune, Jupiter

ESOTERIC RULER: Moon

QUOTE: "Wanna watch anime and discuss our past lives?"

ccording to some people, when you're about to die, your life flashes right before your eyes. You get to see through every glorious high and fucked-up low, and just maybe you get to see through each one of your past lives. If you look at the zodiac as a chronological timeline of birth to death, Aries is the baby, the beginning of life and the zodiac, and Pisces is the end of the line. But Pisces isn't an old person with a hunched back and a bunch of wisdom—that archetype is reserved for Capricorn or Aquarius. Pisces is representative of the twilight years and even embodies something beyond death. Pisces is the unknown, where the soul prepares to leave Earth and set off on a journey with a mysterious destination beyond the horizon of the oceans of dream and space.

To put it more bluntly: Pisces is the most abstract, fucked-up, and least understood sign of the zodiac. Congrats: if you're a Pisces, you're both a baby and an old person. Pisces has the experience and qualities of all the other signs before them, and yet they're still trying to figure out whether their existence in this plane of reality has any meaning at all. They've done it all, and so they understand that the human experience is nothing special—so they can be real downers. However, when they do find someone special, they'll cling to and become obsessed with them. Love, alcohol, movies, sex, and bubble tea: it doesn't really matter. If it can excite them, they'll cling to it like a spider monkey; and if they haven't developed a great sense of boundaries, watch out.

Pisces is co-ruled by fuck-boy Jupiter and sad-boy Neptune. Jupiter is the planet of expansion and abundance, here to make you feel hungry for life and obtain as much as you can from this existence. Jupiter manifests in Sagittarius's personality by making them follow their bursts of passion (a.k.a. horniness) whenever they are sparked; and since Sagittarius is a Fire sign and mutable, it turns Sag into a ghoster and a balls-out risk-taker. Sagittarians are notorious for not being able to stick to the object of their passion for too long, because they are mainly attracted to the rush of endorphins that comes from experiencing something new. They are here for a fun time, not a long time. Pisceans have many of the same qualities; however, they have a hunger for a transcendent experience: they want a sublime rush that proves that their existence is worth something. However, when you are a Water and a mutable sign, the Jupiterian quality manifests as emotional hostage to the energies of this planet. Pisces is the ultimate empath, taking in the energy of whatever room they walk into, the emotion of whomever they are talking to. When they listen to the news, they feel like whatever is happening is as crucial as hell and needs to be addressed immediately—so they are the kind of people who will show up to dinner ready to discourse for three hours about saving the whales without ever asking you a question about yourself.

Co-ruled by Neptune, the planet of forgiveness and salvation, Pisces has a martyr/savior complex. Because they can empathize with the emotions of everyone around them, they feel like the uncaring nature of humanity is what causes so much hurt in this world. Like the thesis of the hit show *Neon Genesis Evangelion*, they register that, if the people of the world could just connect on an emotional level, it would be a better place. However, as *Evangelion* has also taught us, if we were to perfectly empathize with others' emotions, we would lose our sense of individuality in the process and become a giant collective blob of feelings. And, for a Pisces Sun, that is scary. The Sun is all about our individuality and the qualities we are trying to embody, and the Sun in Pisces recognizes the needs of everyone in this world—and desperately tries to escape them. Pisces Sun has a natural struggle to both embody and run away from the emotional intensity of both the world and themselves. That sense of empathy is both a blessing and a curse, because they can get so wrapped up in someone else's pain that they forget where they stand about it as an individual. It is their guiding quality that has them escaping in whatever way they can. The best of these people eventually surrender and place themselves in service to save the earth. The worst of them? Not so much.

Whenever things get overwhelming for them (or, conversely, when they're overwhelmed and bored), they try to get out of their body and transport themselves to a pretty fantasy—or they take themselves to really dark places. Again, escapism tends to be a big part of their personality. They are the dreamers. They wear elf ears to the Ren Faire to act out medieval fantasies, write epic stories about a fleeting crush they had, swear they can read auras, have been known to time-travel into the future in their dreams, and spend a lot of effort dodging energy vampires. Those who have a better handle on this quality eventually use it to bring forth their goals into reality. Pisces is in direct opposition to Virgo, a planet all about work and detail. For Pisces, if they don't jot things down and plan out what they can accomplish, you can bet they'll die in a cluttered apartment under a stack of unfinished novels and half-written poems.

Hopeless romantics. Lost in an illusion of their own making. Crying at the drop of a hat. Detached from reality. Creatures of myth who believe in magical orders and luck. Living in a detached reality where life is kinder and more mystical. Wise beyond their years and ready to leave this earth because they have a soul that has lived one too many lifetimes. If they had a life philosophy, it would definitely be "Get over yourself." Pisceans go through whirlwind romances, die for their beliefs, respect the spirits of the earth. They are overwhelmingly emotional and can let their feelings sail them to the ends of the earth. Pisces may be confused, indecisive, emotionally manipulative, play the victim, and lack boundaries. But all of them share the commonality of having love as their religion and wanting desperately to connect to something bigger than themselves.

PART 2

THE MOON

OUR GOOEY EMOTIONAL CENTER

THE MOON SHOWS OUR EMOTIONAL truth. Our maternal figures. The inner child. The chaotic messes we turn into when we are under duress. How we drunk-text others. How we feel when they drunk-text us. Our Moon sign leads us to our most problematic habits. It contains our coping mechanisms. It shows what we need to regulate ourselves and be present in life. What are those, pray tell? I'll tell you in a bit, so hold up.

14

WHAT LIES
BENEATH

If you've gotten this far, you're the kind of person who has some familiarity with a natal chart. What is a natal chart, you ask? A natal chart is a map of the planets and heavens and where they were at the hour and on the day of your birth. That moment in time is the basis of your chart, a method of divining many of your astrological characteristics by mapping the locations of the stars when you were born. Although the movement of the planets is ever constant, and people born within an hour of each other can have completely different natal charts, the difference is not too strained. Finding your natal chart is pretty easy, as there are approximately four and a half births every second. You can do it online on a variety of different websites. You could even hire an astrologer to do it for you and interpret the results. I'll leave the particulars up to you, but suffice it to say that if you get a copy of your natal chart, you'll be able to find out where the Moon was when you were born, and that will tell you a little more about yourself than just your Sun sign will.

The first thing you must know before understanding the Moon is its glyph, ☾. The circle isn't complete: the shape is similar to this celestial body in its crescent stage. You can find this symbol facing either the right or left—its orientation doesn't matter. What is important is that it's an incomplete circle: not the full picture of the universe, but a fraction of the infinite. The moon on its own holds no light, instead reflecting the light it receives from the sun. The moon exists as the projection of the sun. Its crescent shape, representing the phases of the moon, reminds us that, in the same way, life goes through its phases. The crescent represents either the last phase before a new moon or the phase immediately after it. Just as the new moon represents new beginnings, the glyph reminds us that, out of the unconscious, things are born and things die.

In astrology, the Moon represents the darkness we all surrender to when the light is gone and we are guided by instincts. The Moon is the polarity of the Sun. The Sun is the archetypal father figure, our consciousness, soul-truth, and ego. The Moon is our archetypal mother figure, our id, the inner child, our emotional and immediate needs—basically, it is who we are when we are intoxicated and primarily tuned in to our id. The Moon is all about emotions and memories. The Moon doesn't ask to engage with what's okay for you. The Moon does whatever it can to make itself feel okay.

When you try to learn about the Moon, you can probably come across some online post saying "our Moon sign is who we truly are," or "the Moon is our true self at 2 a.m." I agree with both statements to some extent. But our sole truth is the Sun. The Sun is everything we are trying to be, and it's what we look to when we want to live a more conscious/authentic life. The Moon is the most raw part of our psyche that tells us what we need in order to live and be content. If you're up at 2 a.m., thinking about your emotions and memories, that's the Moon's influence showing up in your life. The Moon is very loud, and when your needs aren't being met, the Moon will take over and consume the Sun. If you are under duress and feel a void in your soul, the Moon will kick in to cope with that feeling of emptiness. If you are a Taurus Moon, you may go on an expensive shopping spree and wake up to find you've accumulated three thousand dollars' worth of credit card debt. If you are an Aries Moon, you might start random arguments just to fight, even though you don't actually care or understand what you're screaming about. If you are a Pisces Moon, you might just disappear into your own world of imagination to evade harsh reality, or get blackout drunk. Or both!

When we look at the Moon, we can't forget about the archetypal mother figure. *Mother* is a loaded word for many people. Some people have complicated relationships with their mothers. Perhaps you didn't have any mother figures when you were growing up and had to be your own mother, or maybe you had the role of a maternal figure filled by someone who didn't fit the traditional meaning of the word. When I talk about the Moon and the mother archetype, think about someone who is there to nurture you, take care of you, make sure your needs are being met, and sustain you when you are hurt. The first five years of our lives often dictate how we are going to emotionally respond to ourselves when we are under duress. When a baby is crying, their mother is typically the first person to respond to their call. Essentially, the role of the Moon is to care for and support our emotional ego. And depending on where we are in life, the Moon will either manifest in a healthy coping mechanism or bring out our most self-destructive tendencies.

ARIES MOON

Did you ever have a friend who would go out for a run whenever he was upset and who refused to talk about it or cope in any other way? Know someone who hooks up with people because they need to let all their frustration out? Or have a family member who always starts fights when she's drunk? If so, you probably know someone with an Aries Moon. In astrology, we look at the Moon to see how we channel our emotional problems when we are under duress. We take after our Moon personality to make ourselves feel good and wholesome.

Aries, ruled by Mars, is bold and expressive and goes hard with their emotions. As mentioned earlier, they are huge babies who feel their needs must be met immediately or else they will completely lose it. They are impulsive and make everything about themselves. They reject any sort of structure or limit placed on them when they are at their most heated. Since they are ruled by Mars, bickering, fighting, and moving around are second nature to them. Act first; ask for forgiveness later: this is the name of the game when you have a Moon in Aries.

TAURUS MOON

In astrology, the Moon changes about every two and a half days. The Moon is moody and hungry to be satisfied. We follow the Moon to see what the collective is feeling and where our emotional ego naturally gravitates, searching for relief. Our emotions don't exactly represent the most stable energy, and two and a half days is not a lot of time, so it can be tricky to pin down the exact manifestation of personality traits in a Moon sign. But, if you were born with a Taurus Moon, congratulations—you have one of the luckiest moons there is to have. The Moon loves being in Taurus, because it is a fixed energy that can contain the ever-changing water of emotions from the Moon.

The Moon is a force of beautiful destruction that comes crashing with all its force onto land. The force of that impact results in a huge mess: when the Moon makes impact with the planet it corresponds to on your natal chart, it instantly spills every emotion it was holding on to. Taurus is a dune, which naturally protects and contains tidal waves of emotions. If you have a Moon in Taurus, your emotional response when you're feeling under duress tends to stay consistent and be manageable. You tend to know how to handle yourself and keep it together so you can go back to being expressive and emotional when the moment is right.

Taurus is ruled by Venus, the planet of beauty, satisfaction, value, and glamour. On Earth, Venus is all about satisfying themselves with the richness that this earth has to offer. They aren't preoccupied with going to war, living their truth, or imposing structure onto this reality. Venus just wants to enjoy a good bottle of wine and enjoy every moment they can while they're alive. They want to eat unlimited breadsticks at Olive Garden and go to a dance party. Moon in Taurus, to extend this concept, satisfies their emotions with things of beauty and earthly desires. Gardens, aged wine, money, scented candles, sex, luxury, spa trips, and/or a hug are all very much appreciated by someone with a Moon in Taurus.

Have you ever known someone who kept running to their ex whenever life came crashing down, kept smoking their cigarettes even when they had a cold, and kept running their credit card even though they only had six dollars in their bank account? If you've known someone like that, it's most likely that their Moon was in Taurus.

There is almost a sad cognitive dissonance whenever Taurus Moons are at their lowest. They need and want their things. It's hard for them to let go of the things that bring them comfort, even when they're the very things causing their own self-destructiveness. They can often treat everything as a transactional treat. No one can buy lasting happiness, but a Taurus Moon is always willing to try.

GEMINI MOON

When you're a sign all about trolling, talking shit, and communicating whatever thoughts are roaming through your head, it may seem like you're a ball of feelings, but Gemini is all about expression with none of the mess. Gemini is honestly one of the most self-regulating signs in the zodiac when it comes to handling emotions, especially as they relate to the needs of others. They may run their mouth constantly, but they're known for being detached. Whereas most people's problem is being unable to express what's on their mind, Gemini has no problem with that. Geminis aren't afraid to talk, ask questions, and explore their thoughts. However, the Moon doesn't do too well under the element of Air. Feelings are found to be cold under Air, which is why it isn't uncommon for Gemini to lay down some brutal truth about even their most treasured friends with robotic precision. They're charming, effervescent, and magnetic—but also somewhat frightening and can come off as uncaring or even, well, a little evil.

Gemini Moons are also known to be flighty with their feelings, going from being super-emotional one moment to relaxed the next. Sometimes it may seem like they have no emotions at all, because all they seem to do is complain. These people are some of the best talkers you can find, known to get into a wormhole of thoughts and theories that can be fascinating if you're into them. If not, listening to them can get tiring—especially once you realize that all the meaty words and existential observations aren't necessarily all that deep. To their fans, they can have the pull of a guru. To the people who hate them, their chatter is pure torture.

Gemini Moon has a lack of understanding of just how they're feeling under duress. Sometimes they know they're freaking out about something, but they're not really sure what it is or why. They like being told how they feel and then deciding if it's how they actually *do* feel. So, as you can imagine, they love a good horoscope, psychological theory, or trendy wellness practice. They're susceptible to political outrage, even though their interest in it can be completely on the surface, and they can be the loudest voice in the room when it comes to any kind of discourse, even if they don't fully understand what they're talking about. They may be the most enthusiastic activists at the beginning of a protest, but don't expect to see them hang out until the bitter end if things get rough. They don't particularly like to get stressed, dirty, or inconvenienced when they can avoid it, and they don't particularly feel any sentimentality when it comes to hanging in there for friends or colleagues.

They tend toward a baseline that is anxious and high-strung, but they thrive in moments of change and uncertainty. While a messy Pisces or Cancer might fall apart when times are tough, Gemini tends toward the cool and clinical when the world is erupting into flames. Just don't count on them to do anything for you if it means potentially breaking a nail, if they aren't wearing the right shoes, or if it's too hot, too cold, the snacks aren't good, and so on. But when they come through, they come through.

CANCER MOON

Home, sweet home. The Moon feels comfortable and in its natural skin when it is in Cancer. Because the Moon represents our emotional responses, our subconscious habits, and our needs, Cancer as an archetype finds itself catering to and following their emotions naturally. Cancer is the sign about how "I feel"—it doesn't find emotional satisfaction by escaping into outer space like a Pisces, and it doesn't find nourishment in talking things out and overanalyzing things like a Gemini. When times are stressful, Moon in Cancer is the sign that goes back home, hugs their childhood stuffed animal, eats ice cream, calls their mother for advice, and then posts up a storm online.

Cancer Moons have a strong connection to their mother, and even as adults they often never go a day without talking to her. However, sometimes Cancer Moons were thrown into a position of nurturing their family, and they themselves have assumed the role of a mother. Then there are some Cancer Moons that never had a strong connection with their mother, or their mothers were missing from their lives. Either way, mothers and family are always something of importance to these people. They can never seem to let go of the presence of their mother or the void their mother left in their lives.

Cancer Moons, just like most Cancer placements, tend to be very reactive with their emotions. They wear their hearts on their sleeves. They blush easily. They smile just as quickly. They have a hard time keeping their face together. However, if they are able to master their expression, don't let any indifferent appearance fool you, as they are very empathetic people. Their emotions are ruled by a celestial body that has no light of its own, so they know how to read the energy around them and project back their own issues like you've done something wrong. If you upset them in any way, they will punch, cry, scream, project, or do breathing exercises in an instant.

Yet despite how temperamental they are, if you have a problem in the world, you can expect a Cancer Moon to be all on top of you. They are the mom friend extraordinaire. They will carry snacks around for when you're hungry, a blanket in case you get cold, and they are always ready with a hug to remind you that someone loves you. Water Moons have almost no escape from their emotions—they're constantly processing them. Air Moons can talk their way into thinking that their emotions are the result of something else. Earth Moons can be productive with their emotions. Fire Moons can let their spirit of optimism delay any processing of uncomfortable feelings. But Water Moons feel every inch of their discomfort, every second of their love. They're doomed and blessed to feel it all.

LEO MOON

Everyone loves a star. The person with their Moon in Leo is that someone: full of charisma. Leo Moon is the big romantic who holds up a boom box outside their crush's window, the first person to make a toast, the narcissist who starts a podcast to talk shit about everyone—in essence, someone with chronic main character syndrome. Many of us assume Leo Suns are the biggest attention-getters, but the shiniest star in the heavens is really someone with a Moon in Leo. Moon signs are easier for all of us to access, since the Moon deals with our subconscious behavior. You don't have to be intelligent about yourself to express your Moon sign—it just happens. Leo Moons are especially powerful, whether you like it or not: they have an undying glow to them and are just naturally louder, bolder, and more glamorous than their Sun counterparts. Sometimes you want to strangle them, but sometimes you're just in awe.

Leo Moons most definitely get their love for the spotlight at an early age. Until the age of five, children set up the emotional responses to stress that will carry them for the rest of their lives. Leos, just like actors, have a special relationship to the spotlight and the ego. As children, they were either given no attention and had to wrestle to get it, or they were given praise and adoration that would rival that of baby Jesus. As children, Leo Moons might have been forced to perform on behalf of their family so they could keep a family image alive, a situation that they either embraced or later resented. Either way, these people were pushed into positions to handle and control attention, regardless of whether they wanted to be seen or acknowledged.

No matter where Leo is in the chart, it is ruled by the Sun: Leo knows how to keep people safe and warm. It also knows how to get people so heated that they want to die. You can either spot a Leo Moon by their dramatic entrances and gestures, or they'll just come up to you and tell you in so many words and then wait for praise. A Gemini Moon is very curious about you, but a Leo Moon is looking to have their reality and opinion mirrored back to them.

Leo Moon tends to have what is medically referred to as Regina George Syndrome—they think they're the best person to have ever existed, a gift from the gods. If you don't sustain whatever special reality they live in, or if you hurt their pride, they won't forget it. Leo Moons are a fixed Fire, after all; they will hold on to the hurt you caused them and find a way to even the score, no matter what. Leos all have a code of ethics, and they have limits to how far they will take things, but they aren't afraid to show their ugliest qualities when they feel it is necessary. Leo Moons, simply put, can be vindictive psychos when pressed, so maybe don't press.

The most highly evolved Leo Moons understand how petty and consuming their emotions can be, so it is possible to be a Leo Moon and not burn down the school when you get passed over for the lead in the musical. Needing others to give you strength, documenting your worst moments for sympathy, using others purely as TikTok props without actual regard for their humanity, maintaining superficial and draining relationships, bringing others down to reclaim your honor, all of it is beneath most Leos. Being a fixed Fire sign, they smolder and sit with their emotions. They have the capacity for self-reflection, even though they may present as self-obsessed jerks. Vanity is a strength to Leos. All that thinking about yourself can give you insight. However, it also might lead to delusions of grandeur, excessive self-hatred, or a sense of righteousness that will help you justify a crusade to slay your enemy.

The Moon represents the inner child. Leo's is a protector of the spirit, the symbol of youth, and above all, very fun. So while Leo Moon has the effervescent energy of an adorable child star, you can also count on them to do the work if they are well balanced. Leo always responds to the Sun, a symbol of truth, and they feel strongly about living theirs. If something in their environment does not align with their soul, they will do what they must to connect back to their essential values.

If there is anything Leo Moon needs to understand in order to master their inner world, it is "stand your ground." Leos are meant to look deep into their souls and figure out just where their heart is, then stand firm with their ideals. Because Leo Moon is a fixed Moon, they are able to hold on to their emotions so that they can better decipher them. That can be a good thing, since Leo Moons often know themselves very, very well (maybe too well), but it also means they can often forget to let things go when they should. Bully them as children, and they will make it their mission to destroy you when they reach adulthood—unless they gain the ability to let bygones be bygones. If they can learn to get over petty slights and feel secure and steady in their convictions, Leo Moons can be great friends, excellent leaders, and overall awesome people. Leo is a fixed sign, after all, and when everyone looks to them for a show, they also look for warmth. Leo Moon may think every criticism, comment, stare, and opinion is personal, but it's often a reflection on someone else's character. A balanced Leo Moon will understand that and continue beaming good vibes even when surrounded by absolute turds.

Leo Moons are just like Cancer Moons in some respects: they see emotions as being personal and unique. Every emotion is just blown out to epic proportions. For a Leo Moon, heartbreaks can actually kill, tension is apocalyptic and can be felt cities away, and their sadness is surely world-engulfing. But no matter what, the show goes on with a Leo Moon. Whether they can deal with their big moods in a reasonable manner or unleash their fury after a sideways look is up to the individual, so just hope that your Leo Moon is evolved. Otherwise, proceed with extreme caution.

VIRGO MOON

Have you ever seen the meme of that confused woman who is doing algebraic equations in her head? Of course, you have. And even if you don't know that meme, you can come to understand that being a Virgo Moon is a life of constant questioning, overanalyzing, and suppressing emotions. Earth and Air Moons have the special ability to not fully feel their emotions all at once; they know how to compartmentalize them. They can catch themselves feeling something and swallow it. As for Virgo Moon, they not only repress their emotions, they break them down. They'll analyze and pick apart the way they feel rather than just *feeling*. Virgo is the nitpicker of the zodiac, after all.

Virgo—ruled by the god of intellect, Mercury—shares a mutual ruler with Gemini. Unlike their Gemini Moon counterparts, Virgo Moons know how to stand in a situation. Gemini Moons regulate themselves by moving on to another topic, thinking themselves out of their feelings, and getting bored with whatever it is that causes them duress. Virgo Moon, on the other hand, wants to know every detail, tracing their steps back to their problem, and will deliberate for hours thinking and talking about what landed them where they're at. The most common trigger for a Virgo Moon is the feeling of not being useful. Virgo Moons need to be at work at all times, which means a lot of unnecessary recitation of facts and stressing about every little detail—all that craziness may not actually help them in the long run, and there was probably an elegant and simpler solution, but by working *really* hard at solving their problems, they're effectively staving off existential dread.

Virgo is the natural ruler of the sixth house, focusing on service, work, and analysis. The way they care for people is by performing acts of service, being at least two steps ahead of other people's needs, and holding space to have long conversations with others. They want to be helpful, they want to work, they want to always talk things out with those they care about. Seems like a great friend to have, a great lover, a great mother—and they can be. But eventually a Virgo may meet someone with a Pisces Moon, or someone who doesn't want to face reality and who faces challenges by pretending their issues never existed in the first place. In that circumstance, a Virgo Moon will keep picking and poking the bear until it unleashes the beast. They just can't keep themselves from being assholes in this way. Virgo Moons have an elephant brain and won't forget. They know every detail about their loved ones. And they can't stand to see them under duress—which sounds great, until they spend hours bugging you when you just want to relax and play some video games to escape your immediate problems.

In astrology, the Moon represents the way you were nurtured, the home life, the mother. Those born with a Moon in Virgo were often nurtured by someone who was critical, anxious, and demanded things be in order and aligned. This person was busy working, taking care of someone who couldn't care for themselves, and overwhelmed with responsibilities. This mother figure may have been anxious about the disaster that would come if one thing went wrong and transferred her anxiety over to her child. This mother (and, again, this doesn't have to be a literal mother but perhaps someone who filled that role) had set up plans about how their child's life should be; and no matter how good it could ever get, it would not be good enough. Head for the hills if something goes wrong.

Virgo is cold in nature under the Moon sign. Virgo parents or caregivers often can't find a way to relate to their children emotionally and instead spend their time and energy making sure their children keep themselves in check. There is hardly time for spontaneous trips to the zoo or theater. Things have to be planned ahead of time, and order is of the highest importance. If this figure is terribly busy working and running or taking care of their responsibilities, they may leave the child to themselves, of course after making sure they are clean and presentable and have everything they could need for their day—although sometimes this figure may go overboard and forbid them to cook or clean for themselves, so that the child won't forget how good and easy their life is because of them.

In astrology, the archetype of Virgo is synonymous with a stepmother. If we think of it archetypally and not literally, we get someone who wanted to provide for you, saw you as a responsibility, but didn't have the appropriate emotional tools to connect in a way other mothers might. First-generation immigrants can often relate to having mothers who operated from a scarcity mentality, counting their pennies—who would kick your ass if you misbehaved but always made sure you had food and someplace to sleep safe and sound.

Having a Moon in Virgo means that you grew up being cared for by someone who didn't let you forget the work they did for you on a daily basis. Virgo Moons can't relax, because they've internalized their mother figure's mentality: they emerged from childhood well cared for but with a gigantic and permanent stick up their ass. The residual drama has left them with a desire to control things when they are under duress, which could mean a nasty mean streak, even if they swear up and down that they care (and they do!). They just need things to go according to plan. At all costs. They criticize their loved ones so they can help them be on their level of functioning. Virgo Moon's greatest strength is a forensic level of interest in pulling apart the details of a conflict, coming back to the scene of the crime to figure out every last molecule that might have led to something deviating from the plan. They want to be useful. They want to matter in people's lives. And they really, really like to be told that they're right. So don't hesitate to praise them, even when you want to escape from them at all costs—it's the best way to make them feel happy and (conveniently) also a great way to get them to stop complaining.

LIBRA MOON

When your Moon is in Libra, you are the chipper, well-mannered, and polite salesman of the zodiac, but also a needy and indecisive mess. The Moon in Libra values airy Venusian qualities: peace, balance, partnerships, glamour, and refinement. Unlike a Libra Sun, a Libra Moon has no problem with being accommodating and can find ways to relate to everyone. However, they can be self-denying and abandon their own needs in favor of someone else's with equal aplomb. Libra Moons hate to be alone, can't stand the thought of losing people, and become indecisive when they are asked to make a decision—how can they choose one way or the other when they would rather have it all?

Libra is a cardinal sign that manifests in intellectualism: they base their actions on logic, not emotion, whenever they are under duress. A Libra Moon doesn't mind talking to friends about their feelings, but they're not really into empathy or give-and-take. If you call a Libra Moon and share your deepest, darkest fears, they'll do their best to relate, but what you might ultimately get is a list of pros and cons, maybe a solution to your problems, or just an invitation to play dress-up and then party all night to show off how well you are. Will Libra Moon push you to face your problem? Maybe not—but you might feel a little better, at least on a superficial level. Libra Moon is the most likely to address a deep-seated emotional issue with a jade facial roller, a couple of cocktails, or a marathon night of dancing and looking awesome. Save the tough emotional work for a different sign.

Venus rules over this Moon, so Libras reach for the following when they need comfort: luxury, goods, money, beauty, and love. Libra Moons are typically hot as hell and have a capacity for being almost impossibly polished. Unlike a Leo, they would never overdress, since they want to be integrated into their environment. They want to look great and not think too hard about what they're doing. But they're typically late to things, since it can take as long as hell to look that good. If you want a Libra Moon to be on time, consider telling them to come to your party two hours before it actually starts.

Our Moon sign is not something we are fully conscious of. It is our instinctual response, a self-soothing mindset typically developed in childhood because of our caretakers or environment. Libra is represented as scales, and, true to form, may have spent childhood as a mediator and felt they needed to balance things in their environment. They are typically very smart people who had to learn to communicate at a young age because they were placed in a position where they had to bring about peace and order to preserve the security of their environment. If you are a Libra Moon, maybe your parents screamed at each other for seemingly no reason, or you were raised around someone angry or unpredictable, and so everyone walked on eggshells. Whatever the reason, you emerged from this environment the consummate moderator, always keeping the people around you happy and festive—or at least keeping things looking like they were all good.

It is also an Air sign: Libra Moons are able to compartmentalize conflict, because if things look good on the surface, why dig in? Maybe you weren't raised in a volatile environment—the other side of Libra Moon starts with a child who was often presented with sweet words, gifts, and affection. Libra Moon is the anxious little baby doll of the zodiac. Venus, that flirtatious ruler, has taught many a Libra Moon at an early age to give compliments, master social skills, and throw around white lies; they'll do whatever it takes to preserve the cotton-candy sweetness of the environment they grew up in. Whenever something bad happens, they revert to people-pleasing, pressuring friends and family alike to put on big smiles and stuff the bad thoughts down.

Libra Moons are *very* conscious of their status and public appearance. In astrology, the part of Libra Moon that rules their emotional life lies in the tenth house. That means they want everyone—friends, family, strangers, people on the Internet—to think they live perfect lives. They measure success through status. They feel that's one of the few ways they'll grow to be secure in life. So expect a Libra Moon to have a perfectly manicured Instagram grid, inhuman adherence to their personal brand, and a life so seemingly full of fun that you question whether they work at all—which is exactly what they want you to think.

The fact is that Libra Moons need the attention of others, and they need to know that they'll keep it. They don't do well on their own, although other placements in their chart could mitigate that. It's less that Libra Moons are dependent and more that they want people around them to be there and make up for what they lack. They know how to pick the best partners for a project, although sometimes in love they aren't so lucky. They can get snobbish and date someone who makes them look pretty and glamorous, instead of being with someone who actually makes their heart rumble. The most mature of this placement will learn to be decisive, be okay with not always looking great, and deal with the most disgusting parts of their shadow instead of running away from it.

SCORPIO MOON

Please keep this information a secret, as we are now talking about the Moon in Scorpio. This was explained a bit earlier in the Sun section, but Scorpio is the second of the Water signs, and they are a fixed Water sign—thus, they embody their element wholeheartedly. That means they're all about emotion. But each of the Water signs experiences and acts out emotions differently. Cancer comes in first and acts out their emotions whenever they experience them. They're impulsive and filter-free, and they have a minimal capacity for anticipating the chaos their feelings may wreak on the unsuspecting people in their orbit. Scorpio, by contrast, is the second of three Water signs: it understands how volatile and cyclical emotions are and is accordingly embarrassed. Scorpios know all too well how powerful and strong emotions can be, but they also acknowledge that they can be fleeting and influenced by external factors, and therefore should be handled as soon as possible. If Cancer is an epic mess, Scorpio is better at keeping their emotions at arm's length, even if they feel them deeply.

In astrology, there are some slices of the zodiac in which each planet prefers not to reside. The Moon dislikes its time in Scorpio. But don't worry if you have a Moon in Scorpio—you're not cursed. The Moon is nurturing. It is the return to the womb, the home, memory, and seat of emotions. Scorpio just doesn't share too many qualities with the Moon. Scorpio is emotion, but it is ruled by Mars and Pluto. Mars is all about the fights, passion, and transformation from action. Pluto is all about survival, the transformation from death, and power. With a sign that deals in intense energy, you can be sure that people who have their Moon in Scorpio are the goblins who hold on to betrayal until death, fueled by revenge. Their "live, laugh, love" is "I'll prove you wrong," applied with extreme prejudice. They're suspicious of everyone they come across and will even notice an acquaintance's slight grammatical faux pas and mark them as an eternal foe. If you want to envision a Scorpio Moon, think of them at 3 a.m., hunched over their phones, trolling the Internet, brooding about the people who have done them wrong. Scorpios are the Moon most likely to obsessively monitor their ex's Instagram page and analyze the reflections in every surface, trying to look for clues. Scorpio Moons are equally likely to create entire conversations and narratives in their heads, fantasizing about epic takedowns of their mortal enemies (who may or may not know they exist). These people love to stay up late thinking about the perfect comeback, imagining the culmination of their epic revenge.

Scorpio Moon has a bit of a reputation for being paranoid. Maybe in their development they were betrayed in some way and have since held deep resentment for people. Or maybe they developed a fighting spirit because they were hurt at some point and swore they would never be hurt again. Or just maybe they had to keep secrets and knowledge that could transform the household. No matter what, they had to learn to hide their emotions in some way from others. They are conspiracy theorists, and they may be way, way too into spreading erroneous memes on social media.

Scorpio Moon is a tragic character in a way; because they never get to escape their emotions, they hold on to their feelings until the bitter end. Of all the signs, their understanding of just how scary the demons under our bed can really be is the most thorough. They see the shadow side that resides in each and every one of us. And there is a kind of upside to that paranoia: they know the darkness of the soul so well that they aren't afraid to have dark and intense conversations. There is a sexiness and strength that comes from people who have this placement. They like to look straight into your eyes when they talk to you, as if they see right past any mask you'd dare to wear. If you ever went on a date with someone who could see right through you, then most likely it was someone with a Moon in Scorpio. That Plutonian influence likes to burn away superficiality and get right to the core of things.

It's a Plutonian and Mars sign, meaning that emotions are meant to be transformed. The most healthy of Scorpio Moons often become artists or use their emotions to help propel them to greater heights. Or at least get them laid. That tortured painter whose work takes everyone's breath away? That smoldering guy with a guitar? That douchebag with a notebook full of edgelord lyrics who unaccountably never runs out of admirers? All are likely Scorpio Moons. They seem to rework every thought that goes through their head into a work of art that can be irresistible to others. And if you think you can whisper a secret to them without it turning into the bridge for their latest song, think again.

With all the hoarding of emotions, they become some of the most intense people in the zodiac. They feel their greatest strength in going where no one else is capable. They like to feel out every extreme and seek experiences that can reach through the dark waters of their soul. But if there is anything Scorpio Moons have to realize, it is that ultimately they must let go of their emotions. If they can't do that, they will have to go through some journey of self-mastery to emerge uncrazy on the other side. They must surrender to their emotions, to the shadow, and face the ghouls living underneath their bed. It's not enough to see through other people's souls if you can't even face your own.

SAGITTARIUS MOON

When the Moon reaches Sagittarius, it produces some of the biggest firecrackers in the zodiac. Ruled by Jupiter, they value expansion and freedom—they're as restless as they come. And these people don't do too well when their backs are against the wall. They need to have an escape route to get out of any situation or they freak the hell out.

Jupiter is all about expansion of the human experience; so, perhaps more than their Sun sign counterparts, Sagittarius Moons are considered lucky. The Moon gives instinctual qualities and personalities that come out at strategic moments: Sagittarius Moon's most crucial qualities are in most evidence when they're under duress. This placement has a natural instinct to trust their intuition, take risks, follow the thrills, and above all, seek out the truth. They all live their lives by a sort of philosophical code, and that can be magnetic. Although they do tend to fuck themselves over by not sticking to things for too long, they make a lot of friends along the way. They just don't feel any particular compunction to keep them or maintain those relationships. Sagittarius Moon views life as a journey, and their mantra is often "the grass is greener on the other side."

Sagittarius is the last of the three Fire signs, and as such, their lives are a journey. Unlike Aries or Leo, they're not interested in identity or their place on earth—they are here to seek out answers and experiences. While their opposite, Gemini, is content just hanging out in their hometown gathering information and asking questions, Sagittarius gets on their horse and heads off into the sunset, led only by the compass of their heart.

People with Moons in Sagittarius tend to be very active. They like going out whenever and wherever they can and hate being caged in. If there's a party invite, they'll escape their teenage bedroom and head off, no matter how strict the curfew. They are the zodiac sign most likely to #vanlife. They do suffer from FOMO, so if they can't get an invite, they'll show up anyway or tell everyone some story about something cooler they did that night. They absolutely can't stand the idea that they might have missed something more exciting than what they're doing at this very second. Therefore, unless they have free rein to follow their nose to the next party/gorgeous vista/new life experience, they sometimes live in a perpetual state of unease.

People with this placement are most likely to have been raised in an environment that had no rules or supervision. Their reckless and spontaneous natures are often a direct result of having too much freedom from birth, whether literal or intellectual. Sagittarius Moons often start life with little to stop them from wandering out the front door and musing about what might lie beyond the horizon. Or, alternately, they were pushed to participate and care about certain ideologies. They may have had parental figures in their lives who were educators, or otherwise taught them to question all their wandering thoughts. This sometimes leads to Sagittarius Moons eventually becoming educators, or at least insufferable know-it-alls.

Or perhaps Sagittarius Moon moved far from their birthplace early in life. Their caretakers were people foreign to this place. Those drastic changes do make someone wonder about foreign lands and begin to explore the possibilities before their peers do. Most importantly, because of that Jupiterian influence, it is very likely they grew up with resources to spare (whether big bucks or just a happy and secure home life) and are accustomed to seeing generosity throughout their lives. These people usually end up with a happy demeanor because they know life is full of abundance, there's much to give, and there's much to get back. They tend to feel that the world is not limited in its treasure.

One thing the Moon in Sagittarius gives to its children is a mouth that kills—not in the sense that they have the best lips in the zodiac (debatable, but that honor would probably go to Scorpio), but rather that their words come to slay. These people value truth above all else, sometimes hurting people's feelings in the process of uncovering it. When someone asks for their opinion, they will give it to them and then some. You want a blunt-force injury caused by the frightening impact of extreme truth-telling? That's Sagittarius Moon. Sagittarius Moon is a natural evolution after the impenetrable walls and emotional retention of Scorpio. Sagittarius is a necessary catharsis. In Sagittarius, the Moon instinctively shoots arrows at inner demons, as well as at the problems out there in the world. This expression of the Moon is all about the truth setting you free.

Sagittarius Moon lives a life of expansion, both in terms of experience and wisdom. You can't ever keep them down for long—they'll pick themselves up in a heartbeat. But though they're always ready with a pro-jectile whenever a problem rears its head, they can often be blind to difficult situations in their immediate surroundings. Because Sagittarius Moon is busy look-ing at the bigger picture, they often neglect to study their immediate surroundings and don't really care about connecting with others. They live a life under-standing that everything is merely a glimpse of some-thing greater. Under major duress, they're the zodiac sign most likely to cause chaos: running over people in a panic, crashing cars, setting stuff on fire. Stressed out a Sagittarius Moon? Get ready for a scene straight out of *Midsommar*. The wisdom Sagittarius has accu-mulated does give them great confidence, but also a sense of superiority that can be deadly. When peo-ple call them out on their issues, their personality flaws, or problems they've caused, they let it blow over (best-case scenario), refuse to take responsibil-ity because they think things will be over and forgot-ten in the long term (less-good scenario), or do what they can to straight-up destroy the offending party (nuclear option). When something goes wrong, Sag-ittarius Moon likes to throw it back to the person who first piped up about it being an issue: if you've got a problem, it must be your fault. They're very invested in not letting others rewrite the heroic narrative in their head. Besides, how could they have fucked up? They understand this world so much better than the people around them.

Sagittarius comfort and safety always lie in wisdom, truth, optimism, and understanding the long game of life. When things go bad, they just turn their gaze toward the horizon, anticipating the destination of their lifelong journey. They love to say yes, be generous with others, and indulge in their excitement. The only thing they can't handle is the mundane conflict of everyday life. They need bigger goals than just being kind to others, taking responsibility for their actions, not setting a building on fire, or busting through a wall in their Jeep. Often they can't escape the narrative they've created for themselves, in which *their* truth is the only real truth. Slowing down, confronting whatever it is that normally makes you defensive, is a struggle for this Moon, but it's also the only way for them to achieve the kind of emotional mastery that can be so elusive.

CAPRICORN MOON

The fabulous sea goat is half fish and half goat. This archetypal being understands and knows the ocean of emotions it left behind to reach the skyscrapers of the world on land. The Moon in Capricorn is not a place for softness. It is also not a place for brooding. It is not a place for boredom. Not even a place for angst. Capricorn hates how weak and distracting emotions can be. They compartmentalize their emotions so they can get to work. They know life can be harsh and cruel, and they're not willing to take any steps back in their life to address it. They'd much rather just see their emotions as a shitty client or annoying responsibility that they have to schedule into their life, rather than something that is a part of who they are. In astrology, the Moon hates being in Capricorn. When the Moon is in Capricorn, it's considered to be in "fall," meaning the planet acts in a way that polarizes our emotions. Capricorn's polar opposite, Cancer, embodies emotions, reacting when the waves of feelings come. Capricorn, by contrast, stands tall when the water of emotions comes rushing forward and keeps moving against the current. It's a busy Moon, so the only function their emotions serve is as steps on a staircase leading toward ambition.

Capricorn Moon is ruled by Saturn, the planet of restriction and discipline. People with this placement were often raised in an environment full of hardships, limitation, loss, responsibility, and maturity. Oftentimes these people came out of the womb as a boss baby, with a diaper in one hand and a briefcase in the other. Perhaps they were born with a lack of material resources or were born in an environment where people were too busy working to raise them. Perhaps they lost a close parental figure at a young age.

Similarly to a Virgo Moon, these people were constantly asked to keep themselves busy at a young age. They may have had to do many chores around the home, be perfect, and perhaps their parental figures also instilled grand expectations of what they could or should aspire to be. People around them pushed them at a very young age to do and be better: live up to the idealized perception of their caretakers, uplift the family status, or live up to the family legacy. Capricorn Moons learn early on that they must shoulder karmic responsibility.

What these people fear more than anything else in life is ending up a failure and not living up to the expectations they've placed on themselves. Capricorn is attached to the tenth house. The house is where you make something of yourself in this world, with the added pressure of your Moon placement. There is a need to seek approval by society's measure of wellness, to feel sustained by who you are and how you feel. Although society's measurement of success seems to always change, these days many of us, especially Capricorn Moon, measure our emotional health by clout. If their lives seem perfect and well on the Internet, they can sustain whatever emotional storm is going on inside them. Expect a Capricorn Moon to have a meticulously curated grid, pristine vacation photos, and an output that offers little aside from a projection of success.

If any of these people ask for a favor out of the blue or invite you somewhere, consider yourself lucky or marked for extradition. Clout-chasers or social climbers, Capricorn Moons have a streak for knowing how to use people. Although *using* is a strong word. Capricorn Moon operates in business terms: when they interact with the world, they clearly define a use and purpose for everything. If they can befriend someone to help them get a good grade, they will. If they can date someone to lift their image, they will. If they have to call their ex so they can get their urges out, they will. These people are very strict with their intentions and what they want out of people—they don't play any games. Just make sure you ask them what they want out of you so there isn't any confusion (on your part).

Though these people have been described as emotionally challenged, they do in fact have a lot of emotions. Like Scorpios, they understand how harsh and debilitating the human heart can really be. Thus, they try to find ways to use their uncomfortable emotions to get ahead in life; however, they can never account for their mysteries, which of course are inevitable. The tragedy of the Capricorn Moon is that they spend so much time trying to harness the power of feelings with brutal indifference and logic without prejudice, but they just can't help but be taken down by their unconscious desires. They can go ahead and categorize and use people, but every once in a while someone or something creeps through their walls, and it can be utterly shattering for even the wiliest of goats.

Capricorn Moons can be sentimental; they can fall in love, and yes, they do have certain attachments that just can't be explained away with logic. However, they don't cave in to those sentimental emotions right away. They could wait around their whole life to find someone worthy to give it all to. Capricorn Moon is the zodiac sign most likely to find their soulmate in a nursing home and spend the rest of their time on this earth enjoying a semi-comfortable spinsterhood.

Capricorns, just like their final-sign siblings (Sagittarius, Aquarius, and Pisces, which are the final signs in Fire, Air, and Water, respectively), are capable of dropping from everyday situations to achieve some bigger goal in life. Failure and laziness get them down. They suffer from a winner's mentality and melancholy. Capricorns want to build something that lasts, they want to defy time, and more than anything, they are scared of being forgotten. Scared of not being able to have a foundation that lasts. And that's their approach to life: when the going gets tough and the tsunami of emotions comes gushing into the towns, they go higher.

Capricorn Moon, as mature as they are, does have the special ability to age backward. Cold as they may

be, many of them do eventually become gushy, sentimental, and playful as they get older. Compartmental-
izing is something they know how to do well, but at the
end of the day, they just want to let everything go. They
know that in order to play hard, you have to work hard.
More than anything, they need earthly stability in order
to feel safe.

AQUARIUS MOON

Here come the biggest goofs, conspiracy theorists,
UFO watchers, futurists, and friendliest robots you will
ever meet. We are talking about people with a Moon in
Aquarius. Under this sign, emotions are intellectualized
and depersonalized. These babes are known for being
eccentric, cool, stubborn, impersonal, rebellious, and
unpredictable. They come off as being either aloof or
cold when emotions are involved. They are the hardest
of all Moon signs to read because they are ruled by two
planets that oppose each other: Saturn and Uranus. Saturn makes Aquarius Moons stern and stubbornly committed to their ideals, while Uranus gives them an air of
rebellion and freedom-seeking. From this collision of
elements, we get a Moon that doesn't care to live up to

anyone's expectations but their own and has their own ideas when it comes to emotional satisfaction. Aquarius Moons value their individuality more than anything, as they often feel people won't understand their emotions. And their engagement with their emotional side can run deep: Aquarius Moons can get so caught up in their inner world that they're completely dead to everything around them. Unlike Capricorn or Sagittarius, other universal signs, Aquarians can get completely lost in their fantasies, whether they're theoretical concepts that may lead to worldwide income equality or steamy fan fiction. Whatever it is, it's not even worth explaining to you: you just wouldn't get it.

Under Saturn's influence, we get a being who practically from infancy was very mature for their age. Though Aquarius Moons are likely to have been born with some limitation in capacity—perhaps financially or emotionally—they tend to make up for their lack of external comfort by holding on to their own ideals to keep them strong. They intellectualize their emotions, so instead of ruminating on how their life sucks, they're more likely to spend time thinking about ways in which they could improve the world.

The Uranus influence in Aquarius Moon indicates that this suckiness may have extended beyond the quotidian difficulties of being a nerd or weirdo, although that may also be true. Aquarius Moons are more likely to have been raised in unconventional circumstances. Perhaps they were born as a refugee, struggled with a rare disease in childhood, or had an unconventional birth. They may have been born during a period of family upheaval or political adversity. Their caretakers may not have been the most consistent people to rely on. Or conversely, maybe their parents were a little too hands-on, teaching them at a very early age to be distrustful and to always question authority figures. Aquarius Moon caretakers? Possibly fringe hippies, counterculture vigilantes, or just scared that the government might be listening in through the cell phone tower in the field next door. In any case, because of this, Aquarius Moons are likely to have been at least partially raised by their communities, which for all intents and purposes includes television and the Internet.

Uranus does tend to give a bit of an unusual vibe to those it influences. Those with an Aquarius Moon, touched by Uranus, tend to be wild cards, operating in high-level concepts and always aware of humanity and where they believe civilization is heading. These people tend to be ahead of their time. They see the grander picture, lamenting that if only the peons around them weren't so selfish or stupid, a utopia might be at hand. As you can imagine, this tendency toward the unique and futuristic is not only an acquired taste, it can make it hard for Aquarius Moons to relate to others. They think no one will understand how they feel, so they often preemptively close up before even trying to communicate their emotions. This tends to result in big supervillain energy for those less well-adjusted Aquarius Moons.

An Aquarius Moon feels most at ease when they are able to express their freedom-seeking self. They like to have the ability to walk around and do whatever unusual thing they can to make themselves feel at ease at any given moment. They love to indulge their whims and fancies for pleasure, but they also have a certain proclivity for epic hatred. If they hate Mondays, they ask themselves why, and they're the people who conclude that what they really hate is capitalism. When they say they hate going to the doctor, they tend to jump right to condemning the medical-industrial complex that makes regular health care inaccessible and prohibitively expensive for the vast majority of people. And while comical and supervillainous extremes are not uncommon for this Moon sign, there is a positive side to this kind of high-concept thinking. The fact of the matter is that we need Aquarius Moons in our society because they point out things we may not normally notice about society and culture. An Aquarius Moon is just as likely to plot the destruction of an entire city as become its most effective urban planner—it just depends on where their mind goes!

PISCES MOON

Pisces Moon: dreamy, elusive, ethereal, a mirror to the thoughts of others, a sponge of emotions. All of them are connected to the realm where dreams, angels, gods, and the dead go to rest. They can connect to every archetypal energy in the glimpse of a second. They can hold empathy for every person and the energy around them. They are also frustrating, drifty, and as impossible to corral as a herd of cats. They may seem fine one moment and then are plunging off the deep end the next. This may be because they're empaths, which means that it's not enough for them to be moody and sensitive as hell—they also pick up on everyone else's shit, too, and claim it as their own.

Many Pisces Moons tend to confuse the struggles and temperaments in their environment with theirs, when those issues actually have nothing to do with them. And if they're not falling apart, they may be known to be aloof, which can be maddening. But their occasional cool moods may not be because they are uncaring or suppressing their emotions. It's just that they are a sea of emotions, so they like to disassociate to avoid being completely swept away by all the nuance and force of those currents. When they are well adjusted, Pisces Moons know how to comfort and relate to everyone. They will go to the ends of the world for their loved ones. It's just that when they aren't in a state of complete alignment, they often lack the proper boundaries. Pisces Moons love mess and also are the mess. Lucky for them, Pisces Moons also do have naturally good fortune. Having a Moon sign connected to so many archetypes, they usually have a special psychic connection to something beyond this realm of reality, and that something helps them not wreck themselves completely even though they're constantly at risk of doing so.

When a Pisces Moon is under duress, they'll often spend days in their room, endlessly binge-watching movies, partying continuously all weekend long, or escaping to the gym for days on end and deadlifting until they can no longer feel their quads. Whatever works; their drink of choice when stressed is escapism, no chaser. In the most immediate of situations, you can find them looking for the quickest and most efficient way to separate themselves from their body, which could include finding the nearest bottle of alcohol to escape the physical world entirely.

These babies do well being alone, but they can also do well when surrounded by people—as long as they force themselves to learn how to separate themselves at least a little bit. But moderation is hard; just like Aquarius, they have a tendency to ghost. They pick up on so much, sometimes it becomes overwhelming. Forgetting the responsibilities and people in their lives, they instinctively feel the urge to dip out when the world becomes too much. Honestly, it's a lucky impulse in some respects, something their Pisces Sun counterpart misses out on. While cruel, ghosting is also an instinct based in self-preservation for a Pisces Moon. Don't worry, though: you can still hate them for it!

Although Pisces Moon is a carer and a sharer with easy access to the full spectrum of emotions—they can even be a little psychic, so keep 'em around for when the Powerball gets to a billion; but they are at risk of users who come in and take their support for granted. They're easy marks for anyone who wants to manipulate their best tendencies: Pisces Moon gets sad for others; they get mad for others; they get vindictive for others. So they're the Moon most likely to carry out a murder-for-hire plot or take on the spiritual responsibility of casting a hex on their friend's ex-boyfriend.

It's in their nature to be a martyr and a savior for other people. They can give and give, but eventually they do run out of juice and feel like they need to get off this planet, stat. In order to make up for this, people who love them should take care to bring some water back into their well to replenish them. Tell them they're pretty, thank them for all they do, and make sure to take care of them when they seem like they're flagging.

That last part can be a pretty unpleasant task, though: they do tend to be a bit whiny and are cool with assuming a state of abject, pathetic misery so people can feel bad for them and give them support. But feed them a snack, pet their hair, and listen to their troubles, and they'll be back on their feet in no time.

Astrology, magick, feng shui, crystals, religion, NFT, bitcoin, and market speculation: anything requiring belief and imagination is something they deeply respect and have a natural inclination toward. Perhaps it's because they grew up in a spiritual household. That might mean one of their caretakers was either super religious or into the more alternative side of spirituality, but that could also just mean they were raised by someone who was an absolute savior, always lending their graces to those in need of help. As a result, perhaps that parent wasn't as available for their own children as they could have been, because other people were in need of help. Maybe they had a parent, like mine, who wasn't in the best shape. They might have had to connect with them through a distance. In any case, Pisces Moon tends to have experienced some kind of distance with their caretakers. To survive and thrive, they had to be empathetic, feel worry, and be concerned about others. And if their home life in childhood sucked, their already wild imaginations would just flourish even more. Pisces Moon always has the energy to dream up a place in their imagination where life is perfect.

15

ECLIPSES:
Don't Text Your Ex
(But Maybe Text
Your Ex?)

Full moons, new moons, eclipses: they're all about destiny, as the famous K-pop starlet Kim Lip once sang. The Moon is our fastest-moving celestial body. In astrology, the universe is mapped in a wheel that is divided into twelve different sections. Think of it as a pizza, and each slice has a different topping. When it comes to your natal chart, the center of that pizza is Earth—in other words, you. Each celestial body has different energy attached to it, and the Moon, as mentioned earlier, is all about emotions. The Moon is the celestial body that moves through the astrological map the fastest, spending about two-and-a-half days in each slice and about thirty days going through the whole astrological pizza pie.

Because the Moon rules over the general public, we can get a psychic insight into where it will steer their emotional attention. If the Moon is in Libra, everyone around you will be desperate to go on a date and not be alone. If the Moon is in Leo, people will be egotistical assholes and will make everything about themselves.

But, when the Moon is full, new, or going through an eclipse, expect riots and breakdowns to occur on every street corner.

In astrology, then the Moon is full, it just means the Moon is the Sun's complete opposite. The Moon is a satellite, so it has no light of its own, and, again, it represents emotions. The Sun blows up all the emotion, shining its light on the unconscious. So when there's no light from the Sun to illuminate the Moon, watch out. All hell is going to break loose. In many myths and urban legends from across the world, we come to understand that people get a bit crazier during a full moon—that's the origin of the word *lunatic*, after all. Breakups are going to happen, cars will swerve off the road, somebody hysterically screaming on the street is going to keep you up all night, the werewolves will come out, and why do you keep hearing bottles being smashed against the sidewalk? It's all reactionary! According to many modern mystics, full moons are a time to manifest. But guess what? The mystics lied. A full moon is the culmination—it is a manifestation in itself, and once it arrives, it's too late for you to will your dreams into existence. The manifestation is already present, and all that is left to do is *be* present to see what piece of information or news is now lit up under the moon's light. The waxing gibbous moon is the phase in which you should write things down and work on your manifestation journal. Manifestation isn't really too sacred or hard to do. It's all about being clear on what you want to bring forward into your life. But if the moon is full? Forget about all that.

A full moon is a frat party: people are drinking beyond their limits, emotions are erupting at every corner, people are letting out their primordial demons to experience the ecstasy of freedom, and deep-seated secrets are being shared so freely, it's like the whole planet is participating in a game of truth or dare.

New moons, on the other hand, can be described as the morning after. Lost in your senses. Hung over. Huge revelations were revealed, and now you wake up knowing life can never go back. Changes must be made. You're stuck in the fortress of emotions, trying to claw your way back to a sense of normalcy. A new moon is when you can step outside the symbolic order. There is no light in the sky—you are stripped of knowing anything that's going on, and all you can rely on are your emotional instincts. Your truth and consciousness are under construction. This is a time when you are facing the void. New moons are often considered to be endings, and they are. In the days before the new moon, you are supposed to throw away things you can no longer hold on to so you can be free. A new moon is a void, and the end of your journey is coming. However, you may not know what that journey is. And you're not supposed to know. All you can do is cry, let go of your chains, and get ready for a new phase of your life to begin.

Now that we know the basis of full and new moons, we have to talk about eclipses. When the moon is opposite the sun, we have a full moon. When the sun is next to the moon, we have a new moon. An eclipse is a new or full moon on steroids. Eclipses typically come in a series of two or three, back to back. What makes this celestial event different from all others is that the combination of the sun and moon is making a connection with the "nodes of faith." We are going to ignore the mythos behind this term, but it's about our destiny and our past lives. When eclipses are around the corner, we feel them two weeks before and continue to feel them for two weeks after each event. Eclipses speed time up. They stir people up. When an eclipse happens, life seems to go into crisis mode and becomes quite unstable for a period of time. The eclipse forces doors open for some people but shuts doors in other people's faces. Unlike other celestial events, these cannot be handled or used for anything. Everything is about destiny during this time. Eclipses have the magical power to bring down kings, raise people into power, and change the direction of where your life is headed.

When an eclipse brings an ending, it's likely to be permanent. New beginnings are harder to see but may be too beautiful to believe. Just remember, eclipses are unstable energy. If an important decision is set to be made, take some time and do it at least eight days before or four days after an eclipse occurs. Everyone is stirred up, untameable, unforeseeable. So the good news is that it's out of your hands; when an eclipse happens, all you can do is pray that faith is in your favor.

MERCURY
GATORADE

J ust a quick note about a planet that we often discuss in casual astrological conversation. Obviously, each planet can affect your Sun and Moon signs, but Mercury is one that comes up often in several contexts, so here's a quick note from your friendly neighborhood Dirtbag Astrologer. I hope in later books we can discuss the others at length!

Mercury Gatorade (or was it retrograde?), Mercury in reverse cowgirl, Mercury this, Mercury that. Mercury's bad, right? This may be the first book you have ever picked up on astrology, but this book probably isn't your first introduction to the astrological side of Mercury. Mercury is a planet you hear about in many different ways. Everyone runs their mouths about Mercury because of its infamous retrograde phase that we will dive into in a bit. This planet is all about thoughts, words, gossip, and information. This is the planet that makes sense of all the information we observe around us. It is the cosmic influence that separates us from the animals. It dictates the way we talk, how we take in information, how we drive, how we learn—and, some may say, dictates our sense of humor.

Mercury is a planet we can look to if we are trying to figure out how our enemies think, or understand what's up with people we just don't get along with. For example, if we look into a Pisces Mercury, we can learn that our frenemy is someone who understands poetic language and likes to connect through abstract words, arts, and dreamy visions. Let's say you can't connect to them no matter how hard you try, and they bug the hell out of you; and let's say you have a Mercury in Virgo. First, you need to know about yourself: you connect to others in a more analytical way, you aren't at all caught up in the abstract or poetic world. Mercury in Virgo is all about making a critique of reality and analyzing everything. The question is, what can a Mercury in Virgo do to connect with a Mercury in Pisces? Well, talk in dreamy and esoteric Pisces language, talk about anything through a dreamy vision, detach just a bit from reality, and communicate everything as if you were remembering a dream. But, conversely, if you hate them and just want to get on their nerves, you can ask them "Is that true?" after everything they say. That's a guaranteed method for driving them insane. Mercury in Pisces people often get caught up in their vision instead of getting to the point.

Mercury movements can also give us a better understanding of our voice and where our thoughts are. For example, when Mercury is in Libra, you may have more productive conversations and thoughts about relationships, fairness, justice, literature, and aesthetics. It's a time when you will probably be thinking about the things you must do in your life to keep yourself balanced. So if you want to write a philosophical social media post that will actually make sense, maybe do it when Mercury is in Libra.

When we look at the glyph for Mercury, ☿, we see a circle with a cross below it and two horns above the circle. The circle represents the Sun/the soul, and the two horns are actually the half circle of the Moon, not actual devil horns. The cross below represents matter and reality. Why does any of this matter? Not sure. As far as I know, it really does not matter. But I'm burdened with this knowledge, and as someone ruled by Mercury, I have to tell you everything! And despite what most people think, no one has the luxury of being uninformed about esoteric knowledge. Billionaires are into conquering the psychic realm, and so you should be too. Back to the topic: the glyph of Mercury can be interpreted in many ways, and it describes how we use our intelligence. We take information from everything that is conscious (Sun) and unconscious (Moon), and we translate it into something we can use to express, understand in a cognitive sense, and grow in our being. Much like Mercury the planet is the connection between our conscious (Sun) and unconscious (Moon) world, Mercury the god is the messenger and guide to the Underworld.

Mercury is also sometimes called the divine trickster. They are the god of wisdom, literature, travel, tricksters, thieves, messages, and transitions. In Jungian psychology, this god is associated with the archetype of the Fool—think of the Joker/Loki/Peter Pan/Bart Simpson/Kevin McCallister. Mercury/the Fool is a being seeking knowledge by any means just for the sake of knowing things, whether that involves testing people's intelligence; breaking apart and picking at concepts, words, and truths; pushing and playing with words and taking them to their absolute extremes; or showing people the error of their thought patterns.

Now we finally get into discussing retrograde. A planet goes retrograde when it *appears* to be going backward. Of course, no planet ever rotates backward, but it can appear that way from our perspective on Earth. When a planet goes backward, its energy goes inward. Think of the planet as going on this continuous journey around the galaxy, but occasionally their spaceship breaks down, so they have to stop and fix any failures that occurred to get themselves back on the road. The planet inspects and goes through the checklist of everything that they may need fixed or improved on so this problem doesn't happen again.

As above, so below. When a planet goes retrograde, we also go retrograde. We become the Joker, and we wreak havoc all over Gotham. We grab our fairy friend and fly off to Neverland. When Mercury goes retrograde, we see the more sinister aspect of Mercury come out. Ghosts from your past start coming back. Laptops start glitching. Cars break down. Secrets spill out. We start seeing things through a different perspective and in ways we haven't seen before. We are not at our cognitive peak when Mercury goes retrograde— we have to think twice about everything and probably feel a little out of it. Mercury goes retrograde about three times a year for about three weeks at a time. And, yes, it feels like hell when Mercury goes retrograde. If packages aren't arriving on time, you accidentally send a risqué text to your crush, your trip gets hit with a delay, and your annoying ex starts calling you out of the blue, it probably does feel like the world is ending. However, remember the Golden Rule: think twice, read twice, and take responsibility for your thoughts during retrogrades. Mercury loves to test people's patterns of thinking. Mercury loves to bring out information you didn't know you had to know. Mercury likes to test you, because at the end of the day, Mercury is a being that lives a life full of knowledge, awareness, and joy. Mercury is all about making sense of this life and giving everything a fuller meaning, and meaning is sacred. So even if Mercury retrograde makes you absolutely want to die, hang in there and try to see it through—there's a benefit to all the madness.

CONCLUSION

Over the last decade, astrology has spiked in popularity. There are plenty of reasons why: worldwide chaos and uncertainty, societal change, memes. And regarding that last piece, perhaps it's because of the compact nature of memes that we are able to reflect on our behavior and insecurities so quickly and easily. The comfortable structure of a familiar image and quippy message speaks directly to our anxieties in this ever-changing world. It's a super-efficient package for delivering wisdom that people understand and that simultaneously gets under their skin. Or, memes aside, perhaps there are simply more people waking up to the cosmic coincidences all around us. Who's to say! Whatever the case may be, the renewed interest in the movements of the stars certainly gives insight into what the human experience has in store for us. The more we reach out in search of understanding, the closer we get to it through trial and error and individual soul-searching.

Astrology is a practice of empathy, a study of character, a study of the mind, a study of the human will, a study of being present. Astrology, although it has been monetized and ripped apart from its magical origin, is still a tool of magical practice. Astrology is fascinating and surprising, and it is a great way to call out the assholes around you (and the asshole closest to you: yourself). By understanding the constellations providing energy to those you hold closest, you can have a better understanding of your world. In this book, we've mostly dived into the Sun and Moon. These energies are the easiest to understand and serve as some of the most important components of our being. The Moon is our emotional ego, the mechanism for interacting with others, and our most natural/unconscious personality. The Sun is our soul truth, the archetype we are striving toward, and the core of our being. Figure those two things out, and you can easily get the general picture of yourself or someone else. For example, a Scorpio Sun with a Virgo Moon: this person is secretive and intense, naturally very critical and calculated about everything. They like to analyze and fix the things around them, they hate dealing with surface-level problems and issues, and they seek out experiences that touch their soul. That's a great beginning for trying get to reading someone: the core of their truth (Sun), and the emotional personality that comes up when they interact with the world (Moon).

The planets represent the different energies of this worldly experience, and the signs give texture and further meaning to those energies. For example, Mars is not just a planet, it is also a point in our psyche and the collective unconscious that represents anger, wars, action, and passion.

One of the most important occultists of the twentieth century, Aleister Crowley, defined magic as "the Science and Art of causing Change to occur in conformity with Will." Crowley believed magic was the interruption or action taken to upset the natural flow of nature and bend it to your own will. According to this definition, many things can be considered magic if you take action and combine that action with willpower. *Anything* can be a magical act, if you only were to have an added bonus of intention and fuel for your action. Drinking, dancing, texting, screaming into the void? All magic, if you act with intention.

In the midst of the global pandemic that was still raging while I wrote this book, I looked to find more clarity on the occult and the mysteries of the world and came across the work of Alejandro Jodorowsky, *Psychomagic.*

This book details a bit of the history of magic, as well as the underbelly of all those magical acts. For example, people can boil a cat, extract oil from the flowers they've been growing for months, and shave off all their hair, then mix it up to create a love potion. The potion is so strong that it causes anyone who drinks it to fall in love at first taste with the person who gave it to them. Let's say you go forward with a potion like that—you give it to your crush, and they're instantly enamored of you. Why is that? You can choose to be satisfied with the explanation that it is magic. However, according to Jodorowsky, the "real magic" was the making of the potion: doing a monstrous thing like boiling a cat, cutting your hair, and destroying flowers you've been growing for months. Somewhere, as part of the process, parts of your psyche were pushed to their limits, your shyness may have burned away, and you gained a confident IDGAF attitude. By the time you gave the potion to your crush, you had a new attitude about romance; your shell of insecurity drifted away; and you began to hold your head high with confidence. That new sense of self, that change in your psyche and attitude? *That* was the real magic. The potion was just the tool that helped you transform. Your crush didn't know what was in the potion, but your confidence when you gave them a drink touched their heart, and they noticed enough to see you in a beautiful new light. The real magic was the *process*—it was never about the potion.

Astrology as a magical tool can serve many purposes. You can look at a birth chart—whether it's for a building, a movement, or a person—and see its personality and the type of energies it would attract. In this way, you can get an understanding of its history and intuitively know how to interact with it. Scared about where your country is headed? You can look at the horoscope of a nation, and you can get a psychic understanding of the temperament and motions it is going through. Feeling like a hermit after months of lockdown? You can use astrology to get closer to people. You can use astrology to set up the perfect time to ask your boss for a raise. You can even use astrology to find things you have lost. And though most examples I just mentioned are possible, it is stuff for more advanced studies—so take this as an appetizer and look for meatier sources of astrological and magical information if it whets your appetite.

One thing to note: astrology isn't divination. Astrology is a language filled with a collection of keywords. Nothing is *destined* to happen. No one is set to have a certain personality. You can predict and assess the personality of a being using broader words. However, everyone has in their head their own individual path to becoming the person they want to be. Some people run away from who they want to be. Some people are the full embodiments of their astrological charts.

The Sun and Moon are the most prominent and biggest psychic influences on our lives. They are some of the most important energies to learn and understand if you want to take your astrology knowledge anywhere. Everything else will come in due time. The Sun is not only the center of our universe—it also centers our constellation within us. The Moon, the celestial body that orbits around our planet, is the energy that revolves our own inner constellation to guide us and keep us safe.

Due to time and other supernatural occurrences, I could not dive into sharing further astrological knowledge. At some time, perhaps, this book will have a sequel, and in it, perhaps, I will add more dirt on each sign, and perhaps certain demons I made deals with will let me spill their astrological secrets. Till next time, I'm blasting off.

ACKNOWLEDGMENTS

To the stars, the Sun, the Moon, God, and the rest of heaven above, thank you for allowing me to exist in this space and time.

To my mom, whom I dedicated this book to, thank you for letting me watch documentaries of Nostradamus as I was growing up. Thank you for always reading me books on ancient mythology. Thank you for telling me stories about the supernatural world. Thank you for always trying to solve every existential question I had as a child. And thank you for your support and psychic visions. As far as I can remember, you made me believe how magical this existence is.

Thank you to my dad, dog, and siblings. Your willingness to support me and be the guinea pigs in my occultic experiments will not go unnoticed.

To my editor Kate Zimmermann and Union Square & Co., I am eternally grateful. This book wouldn't have happened without your work and support.

I could give thanks to the whole world for making this book possible. But I'll be narrowing it down to every single one of you who gave me support, guidance, and inspiration throughout this book process: Liana Mack, Annabel Gat, Hannah Mickool, Danny Larken, Alejo Agudelo, Monisha, Snake Channeler, Donald D'Alessio Andy, Shey, Rana, Jan, Bri, Kitty, Devin, Jake, Alexis, Cesar, Hafsa, Planet Dirtbag, Comfortland, Wellbutrin, iced lattes, and every being who has ever followed @gnarlyastrology.

ALBERTO "ALBY" TORIBIO is The Astrology Dirtbag, a well-informed and lovingly caustic guide to cosmic wisdom. He runs @gnarlyastrology, a popular astrology account beaming memes and life lessons to its more than 200K followers. Alberto has been interviewed in *Vogue*, Buzzfeed, *Cosmopolitan*, and more. He lives in Queens, New York.